UN
CANCELED

ALSO BY PHIL ROBERTSON

Happy, Happy, Happy
UnPHILtered
The Theft of America's Soul
Jesus Politics

UN
CANCELED

FINDING MEANING AND PEACE
IN A CULTURE OF ACCUSATIONS,
SHAME, AND CONDEMNATION

PHIL ROBERTSON

NELSON
BOOKS
An Imprint of Thomas Nelson

Published in Nashville, Tennessee, by Nelson Books, an imprint of Thomas Nelson. Nelson Books and Thomas Nelson are registered trademarks of HarperCollins Christian Publishing, Inc.

Published in association with Yates & Yates, www.yates2.com.

Thomas Nelson titles may be purchased in bulk for educational, business, fundraising, or sales promotional use. For information, please email SpecialMarkets@ThomasNelson.com.

Library of Congress Cataloging-in-Publication Data

Names: Robertson, Phil, 1946- author.
Title: Uncanceled: finding meaning and peace in a culture of accusations, shame, and condemnation / Phil Robertson.
Description: Nashville, Tennessee : Nelson Books, [2022] | Summary: "New York Times bestselling author Phil Robertson delivers a blueprint for standing up for the truth of Jesus Christ in a culture that has forgotten how to have respectful conversation and often suppresses conservative opinions and biblical values"-- Provided by publisher.
Identifiers: LCCN 2021041777 (print) | LCCN 2021041778 (ebook) | ISBN 9781400230174 (hardcover) | ISBN 9781400230198 (ebook)
Subjects: LCSH: Christianity and culture. | Cancel culture.
Classification: LCC BR115.C8 R634 2022 (print) | LCC BR115.C8 (ebook) | DDC 261--dc23
LC record available at https://lccn.loc.gov/2021041777
LC ebook record available at https://lccn.loc.gov/2021041778

Printed in the United States of America

22 23 24 25 26 LSC 10 9 8 7 6 5 4 3 2 1

I dedicate this book to my fellow soldiers who wage war against falsehood and are attacked by the cancel culture world for speaking truth. I hope that by reading this book, you will be emboldened to calmly stand firm and continue to hold up the Son of God as the embodiment of truth. I pray that you will never waver on this because he has promised us victory over every pretension that sets itself up against the knowledge of God.

CONTENTS

A *Note to the Reader*. ix

Preface. xiii

Introduction xxi

Chapter 1: What Is Cancel Culture?. 1

Chapter 2: Where Did Cancel Culture
　　　　　Come From? 21

Chapter 3: Who Participates in
　　　　　Cancel Culture? 43

Chapter 4: Why Is Cancel Culture Happening?　61

Chapter 5: Who's the Boss? 77

Chapter 6: There's a Vaccine for That! 91

Chapter 7: Jesus Cancels Guilt and Shame . . .101

Chapter 8: Check Your Passport 111

Chapter 9: I Ain't Afraid of No Ghosts! . . .123

Chapter 10: The Perfect GPS 135

Chapter 11: Who Are You to Tell
　　　　　Me What to Do? 147

Conclusion: The Gospel: We Are Unashamed 167

Notes　　　　. 179

About the Author 185

A NOTE TO THE READER

I want to sell books, but I also want to be honest with you: this book may not be for you. If you are comfortable with the current cultural climate that feeds off of anger and personal attacks on others, maybe you should take a pass on reading this book. Or maybe you should read it—perhaps it will spark something in you that will help you see that if we continue on this path, America (and the rest of the world) will wind up destroying herself.

On the other hand, if you are one of the millions of Americans who are depressed, frightened, anxious, and a little bit angry about what is currently going on in our beautiful country, I want to speak with you about that because I'm with you. I don't like what I see one single bit. Not at all. Like you, I'm concerned about what America will become over the next few months and years, and I want to do what I can to help us change course.

I am a patriot, but I'm not writing primarily as a patriot. I am first and foremost a follower of Jesus Christ, who died for my sins and was raised from the dead. As a result of the commitment I made to imitate him, I want to make sure I respond to the current political and social climate in the same way he would respond. And that's why I've written this book—to encourage us all to seek him and his wisdom as we navigate the swamp that our culture is becoming. The argument I make in this book is that we all have two choices. Either we can rely on our own understanding—which will lead us to more depression, anger, anxiety, and fear—or we can seek God and his wisdom. In my humble opinion, that's the only path forward for me. I can find peace nowhere else.

PREFACE

I've been wandering around this planet for over seventy years. For the first twenty-eight years, I was meandering aimlessly; I had no direction and no endgame in mind. I guess you could say I was just living day to day. I never thought about politics except to pass judgment on politicians. "Hey, they're all alike! Crooked as snakes." I also tried not to think about the Almighty, even though it was difficult to ignore him when I was in his creation pursuing wild game and fish. Instead, I was mainly focused on satisfying the desires of my sinful heart. One more bottle, one more woman, one more joint—that's what I thought about.

Still, even though I was oblivious to the direction of politics, religion, and culture, it did not escape my attention in the 1960s that people were in the streets to protest one thing or another. It seemed like the world was on fire. In some cases, it actually was. Cities and college campuses across America were erupting in violent social unrest. Rocks, firebombs, and gunfire threatened to destroy us. Folks seemed more violent and fearful than they had been only a few years earlier.

Looking back, it's now obvious that some things just weren't right in America. For one thing, we were in a war we weren't committed to winning. Our boys were being drafted into the army and sent halfway around the world to lay down their lives, and most of us didn't even know why. Many of you know my brother as Uncle Si, but in the late 1960s, he was just a fresh-faced kid who had the misfortune of having his number selected in the draft lottery. The stories he told about the half-heartedly fought war gave me some insight into why people were reluctant to get behind the effort.

Another fire was also smoldering in our country at the same time. In the early 1960s, black Americans began to rise up and articulate their demand that America make good on its promise of life, liberty, and the pursuit of happiness for them too. Until then, they had suffered under a two-tiered system that denied them equal treatment. I clearly recall the separate-but-equal doctrine in place in almost every Southern state at the time. It promised to bring equality of opportunity and government access to all people while maintaining ethnic segregation. By law, African Americans were served by different schools, they had different entrances to hospitals and theaters, they drank from different water fountains, and they used different bathrooms. Economic and employment opportunities were separate too. Separate but unequal!

The problem was, while the promise to keep things separate was kept, the promise to make things equal never materialized. For instance, black children learned from hand-me-down books that had been worn out in white classrooms. The restrooms reserved for black people were usually outside, at the back of filling stations and convenience stores, and were rarely cleaned or stocked with supplies. The best medical care was reserved for whites.

For many reasons, the 1960s were a chaotic and angry time, trust me. People were simply tired of the lies, empty promises, and corruption of government. They had grown weary of injustice and inequality, so many took to the streets. It was a rough period in our nation's history, I can tell you that.

In many ways, the climate in America today may seem to mirror what was going on then. But I think most of us sense that something else is taking place that makes the sixties and seventies seem calm by comparison. In that era, if someone demanded an end to the war, for example, we might not agree, but we understood they simply thought the Vietnam War was immoral and our troops should be brought back home. Even if the most ardent racist in the sixties was unwilling to admit that segregation was evil, at least he understood what African Americans wanted. Most people had a sense of right and wrong, even if their view of morality was inconsistent. At least we understood (in theory) that evil was very different from good. Most of us were clear about that.

But now? I am aware that people are irate, and I think I understand why. The difference between today and the sixties, though, is that a lot of the injustices that cultural zealots claim to be enraged about just don't make sense today. The rage in contemporary America doesn't seem to be connected to any ideas of objective right and wrong. Instead, I suspect too many Americans are just plain angry and are looking for someone or something to take it out on.

Take, for example, James Corden, who used to have a segment on *The Late, Late Show with James Corden* on CBS called "Spill Your Guts or Fill Your Guts" in which he asked personal questions of famous guests. If they refused to answer, they were required to eat something gross. When Jimmy Kimmel refused to answer a particular question, he was offered a choice between several exotic foods that included a balut, a steamed fertilized duck egg popular in the Philippines.

A TikTok user took offense at the segment in which the late-night comedians' description of the balut was "horrific" and "really disgusting," saying the pair were "incredibly culturally offensive and insensitive." She accused the men of encouraging "anti-Asian racism."[1] Corden was then targeted with criticism and a petition circulated to cancel the segment. It was canceled.

While balut may be a popular food among Filipinos, it probably won't make the menu at the Cracker Barrel. Most Americans would actually find the thought of eating a fertilized duck egg repulsive. And, hey, I get it. Miss Kay once posted a video of her preparing fried squirrel meat. You would be shocked to find out that people in other parts of our nation find fried squirrel to be "horrific" and "really disgusting." While squirrels might be a delicacy here in Louisiana, eating them apparently isn't wildly popular in the Bronx.

The question is, does being repulsed by the prospect of eating fried squirrel meat fuel anti-redneck hatred and racism? Is it a serious assault on my culture? Should I be offended? In my opinion, if George and Betty from New York City refuse to ingest the fried rodents I have prepared for them, then that can only mean one thing: there's more for me to eat. I'll just fix them a peanut butter-and-mayhaw-jelly sandwich.

Honestly, I don't think this lady is really convinced that Asians will be disrespected because Corden and Kimmel turned their noses up at balut. I don't think that's what she's really mad about at all, and she has been quoted as saying she mainly wanted to hold Corden accountable. But I think it all comes down to this: too many people are so dissatisfied with a life driven by consumerism and the pursuit of pleasure that being angry at least makes them feel alive. Being enraged gives a false sense that we have significance in a world where we feel insignificant and anonymous. I think it's clear to most folks that an angry, crusading life compelled to burst out in anger at the slightest perception of injustice is a life that will never find what it searches for. That person will never be fulfilled.

I'll make the case that a God-centered worldview is the only path to significance. My message is clear: people are hardwired to find fulfillment only in a trusting relationship with the God who created and died for them. Nothing else answers the question of why we are here and where we are going after we die.

Furthermore, nothing else can give us a meaningful framework for living joyfully in a world that is so full of injustice, violence, and hatred. Nothing else can offer emotional and spiritual peace in a culture that is increasingly committed to canceling folks who step out of line. My worldview insulates me from all of this. God is real! He loves us! He sacrificed for us! He's coming back for us!

The reason I'm so concerned about the impact of cancel culture is that it has the potential to escalate from words to physical force to impose its worldview. And we are already seeing this shift take place. According to statistics provided by the FBI and reported in the *New York Times*, violent crime was up 24 percent in large cities by June 2021, which is on top of a 30-percent rise in violent crime in 2020.[2] This is not a good sign, America. Unbridled anger must have an outlet, and when words fail to provide the adrenaline rush we crave, the only alternative is to put our words into action, violent action. Are any of us comfortable with the notion that, when we don't get our way, we just knock people in the head and take control by force? I hope not. But the evidence seems to be pointing to the possibility that this is where we are.

One of the most bizarre cases of irrational anger boiling over into even more irrational violence occurred in Memphis in June 2021. A Burger King customer ordered a spicy chicken sandwich and discovered the sandwich had too much hot sauce on it. After losing the argument with the employees, she went to her vehicle, where a male friend was waiting for her, and they opened fire on the employees from their car.[3] I wonder if the couple had a conversation in the parking lot such as, "I don't get stirred up about a lot of things, but this is one issue I think we should take up arms over. I'm willing to kill or die for a spicy chicken sandwich." Thankfully, they were bad shots, and no one was killed.

Unfortunately, incidents such as this are becoming far too common. None of this bodes well for the future of our republic because the fruit of this outrage and hatred is that we are in danger of imploding as a society. No family, no community, no nation can withstand prolonged attacks on itself from within. Sooner or later (and I'm afraid it's sooner), the fabric of our nation will be permanently shredded, and we will not be able to reverse the damage. I desperately hope I am wrong. I truly do.

INTRODUCTION

It was in the fall of 2013 that one of my more politically aware relatives burst into my home late one Wednesday evening. I could tell he was agitated. He's a little high-strung.

"If you don't back down," he said, almost out of breath, "you will have a platform to preach the gospel like you wouldn't believe." I've written about this before, but let me give you the *Reader's Digest* version.

I knew exactly what my relative was talking about. It was all over cable news. CNN, MSNBC, Fox News, all of the alphabet channels. They tell me the internet was ablaze with it too. Preachers were already preaching about it in their Wednesday night services. People who supported me were posting about it on social media. So were the people who hated me (and there were plenty of those too). The talking heads on cable news railed against me. Within a single hour, I was in the national spotlight in a way I had never anticipated.

It began innocently enough, that's for sure. A few weeks before, a young writer for *GQ* magazine had sat across the living room from me and quizzed me on my views about various topics.

To be honest, he could have saved himself some time. A quick glance around my living room should have been enough to tell him what I was all about. To begin with, next to my chair, on a coatrack, hung a fully loaded AR-15 within arm's reach, ready for action. Adorning the walls of our humble abode were Miss Kay's Bible verses painted on slabs of rough wood that looked as if they'd been simmering in the muddy waters of the Ouachita River for a hundred years.

"For God so loved the world that he gave his only begotten son."

"As for me and my house, we will serve the Lord."

Then, next to my rather large recliner (the one covered with trendy camouflage fabric), lay my well-worn Bible, held together with duct tape. Everything about the appearance of that book should have made it clear to the young man everything he needed to know about me. *This man reads his Bible a lot!*

Yes, the evidence of who we were was everywhere in our house. He didn't have to interview me. It should have been apparent. We are God worshippers. We read and believe his Word. And we make it our aim to please him, to rely on the one who raises the dead. If God speaks it, we always go with what he says.

No doubt about it. There should have been no ambiguity at all about who I was. But he asked his questions anyway. Finally, he got to the one that poked the hornet's nest. Standing nonchalantly before my recliner, he asked, "Phil, do you believe that homosexual behavior is a sin?" I realize now that it was a setup designed to marginalize any influence on our culture I may have had. What he didn't know was that I was willing to be roasted by the press for telling the truth.

There's no way the young reporter could have known this, but I had spent the last four decades poring over God's Word, the Bible. I didn't set out to memorize Scripture; it just happened. I had become so familiar with it by repeated study that large chunks of Bible passages were firmly committed to memory. So when he asked my opinion about homosexuality, I didn't actually give my opinion. I simply gave him a Bible verse. He just didn't know it was from the Scriptures; he thought I was just spouting off at the mouth on the subject. It was at least two weeks before the media figured out where my words were from:

> Neither the sexually immoral nor idolaters nor adulterers nor men who have sex with men nor thieves nor the greedy nor drunkards nor slanderers nor swindlers will inherit the kingdom of God. (1 Cor. 6:9–10)

That's it! That's all there was to it. A simple Bible verse that set the cyberuniverse on fire.

By the time the article was in print, they made it sound like I had equated homosexuality with greed, alcoholism, and swindling, that I had just pulled an opinion out of my hat. In the reporter's mind, and in the minds of those who don't know God or his Word, I immediately became a bigoted, self-righteous religious zealot, a new age neanderthal. I remember watching a minister on Fox News offer his opinion on my violation of the PC/cancel culture rule. I don't remember exactly what he said, but it was something like, "What do you expect from some redneck living in the swamps of Louisiana? He's certainly no theologian!" He didn't know I had quoted a Bible verse either. To all of them I was a relic of a past that should be cast on the ash heap of history, right along with Hitler, Stalin, and Pol Pot. There's no place in today's enlightened world for the likes of me. At least according to them.

It's worth noting I had included verse 11 in my response to the reporter:

> And that is what some of you were. But you were washed, you were sanctified, you were justified in the name of the Lord Jesus Christ and by the Spirit of our God.

I explained that homosexuality was not unlike any other sin. I also went to great lengths to share the message of Jesus and how all sin can be eradicated by simply putting our faith in Christ. In fact, I spent several hours with the young man, showing him around my land and letting him fire a gun for the first time, all the while preaching the gospel to him.

As I said, it was a setup, a trap I was willing to fall into. But did I hate the man for it? Was I angry? Did I try to retaliate against him? Hardly! I just loved the guy because I knew he was under the influence of the one who had once controlled me. He didn't know what he was doing, not really. He wanted to cancel me, but I only wanted to introduce him to the one who could give him eternal life.

You may be wondering what price I paid for telling the truth about God's will for humanity. The short answer is that it cost me a cool ten million dollars! That's the price we paid for my simply quoting a verse from the Bible. But before you get all stirred up about it and come to my defense, I have to tell you one thing. I would do it all again. It was ten million dollars well spent. It didn't slow me down one bit. The way I figure it, Jesus paid with his life for telling the truth. The only thing it cost me was a few bucks. No big deal.

I don't recall the term *cancel culture* being used at the time, but the forces that lined up against me would later be identified as just that: the cancel culture. At the time we just figured the "thought police" were ramping it up. What's going on today is the same as what happened to me, only it's a much more powerful force at work now than in 2013. Power brokers in academia, the media, politics, and the corporate world have amassed an incredible amount of power to squash anyone who doesn't toe the line, and they are now running with a full head of steam. Since they are winning the war, I think it's critically important for us to know who they are and what they're all about.

We may not win the public relations war by convincing the masses to love (or even like) us, but we can win the personal war—the real war—by not falling for their well-conceived strategies designed to intimidate the masses into submission to their god, the god of political correctness. They have one clear goal: to shut you up or destroy you or both. That's it! That's all they're after.

It's also important to understand what they are all about because most of their victims won't even know what hit them until it's too late. In my case, I was unceremoniously fired within hours of the GQ magazine hitting the shelves.

One of the network bigwigs called me and apologetically said, "Now, Phil, we didn't fire you. We just placed you on a temporary hiatus."

My response to him was, "Hey, Jack, I looked up 'hiatus' in the dictionary and it says 'not a part of the program.' Oh, I've been fired, all right. But do you hear me complaining? Have you heard a word from me?"

In my case, I had already made up my mind that I would not be surprised at anything they threw my way.

In spite of all the negative publicity, and in spite of the tremendous pressure exerted on me to take back my words, I didn't. Truthfully, I could not take it back, even if I wanted to, because those weren't really my words at all; they came from the throat of God Almighty. How could I have apologized for quoting the Creator? So I simply stiffened my back, knowing I was speaking with authority because I had spoken the Word of God.

Oh, they tried to cancel me all right, but their efforts came to nothing. Instead of shutting me up, I became even more vocal about the truth of Jesus Christ. My heightened commitment to speak truth was driven by a newfound awareness of exactly who my opposition was, who they were actually working for (the Evil One), and what they were up to. There was no way I would cave in to that. Ever.

As a result of my experience, I speak with authority on this movement, on the goals and strategies of the cancel culture. I'm not being arrogant here, because my authority is not my own. For one thing, my authority comes from the fact that I am well familiar with God's Word. I know him! I know what he says! I know these things not because I'm smarter than the average person or because I have a special conduit to the Almighty but because he's revealed them to me. In fact, he's revealed his truth to all of us. It's accessible to everyone, even to the members of the cancel culture crowd.

And second, my authority comes from experience, the experience of being the object of their desire to cancel me. I know these people. I know their view of the world is far different from mine, which is centered in the truth that an eternal God spoke everything into existence. It is firmly centered on the truth that we were all created in the image of God and that all people are important because of that fact.

I began working on this book in the midst of the pandemic that began in the spring of 2020. At the time, the presidential election was beginning to take on a life of its own. Anyone who was keeping up with the events of 2020 could see a welling tide of anger heading toward us with increasing velocity. We knew—at least most of us knew—this wave would reach America's heartland and destroy what little was left of our love for our country and for one another.

At some point I turned away from a cable news show I was

watching and told Miss Kay, "This thing is about to get out of hand." People from both ends of the political spectrum were attacking the other side with lies and unsubstantiated rumors. The language from both sides was often vulgar and degrading. Leftist radicals were setting fire to cities all across the country, and right-wing radicals were threatening bloody revolution. I imagined a large powder keg with people from both sides fighting for the honor of being the first to light the fuse. It was a new and frightening experience for me, and I'm old enough to have lived through the unrest of the sixties and seventies, so that's saying something.

I was left with one tormenting thought: without a doubt, America is in peril. I'm no prophet, but I had already experienced the wrath of this crowd years before. I knew what was coming, and it wasn't good.

Soon after the election, the two sides dug in their heels and began to attack each other with a new kind of viciousness. Now, instead of just the extreme Left taking to the streets in waves of violence and destruction of property, the extreme Right briefly got in on the party when they invaded the Capitol and threatened the safety of the lawmakers and their staff.

Soon after that event, I said on my podcast that you won't find me scribbling slogans on a poster board, nailing it to a stick, and marching in protest. Nor will you find me spraying the f-bomb on buildings and road signs. You'll never see me giving the middle finger to anyone; I don't care how much I disagree with them. I made the point that the problem with America is that we have a spiritual disconnect, that too many of us have abandoned the love of God. I pointed out that the result has been that we've put our hope in human constructs like *secular education* (indoctrination), *churches that have drifted away from the simple message of the gospel*, and *partisan politics*. But the problem isn't political or religious, at least not in the sense that religion has come to mean an allegiance to an institutional denomination. Those are just symptoms of a much more serious disease. Our problem is spiritual, rooted in our nation's drift away from the knowledge of God. As Paul said in Romans, too many have embraced the idea that the knowledge of God just isn't worth it (1:18–32).

As a result I have zero hope we can correct what is wrong with us by electing the right person to lead us. Besides, politics is only a reflection of the culture as it already is. It's a mirror of the reality going on all around us. Having said that, I am still hopeful that God will lead our nation to bow down before him again so we can enjoy a few more years of liberty.

That was the gist of what I said on the podcast. I'm happy to report that thousands of listeners thanked me for pointing out that my allegiance is first and foremost to the King of kings, that I am a citizen first of the kingdom of almighty God. They had been looking to the Right and then to the Left for someone to restore some sense of order to the chaos, but they weren't finding anyone. They hadn't considered there could be a third alternative. It never occurred to them the solution wasn't in the middle. So I encouraged them to give up on looking left and right and to look up instead. They had been thinking in linear terms, as if all worldviews were in a straight line. But the Right and Left extremes were one and the same, in my opinion. Both extremes had made the same mistake: they had placed their hope in human institutions and humanistic reasoning. Both were flawed for the same reason. No God!

So when I spoke about this on the podcast, I pointed to neither Joe Biden nor Donald Trump. I pointed to Jesus instead. As I said, most of my listeners thanked me. But this time a few of those on the Right were the ones to attack me, to cancel me. I don't recall exactly what they said, but it was close to "You traitor! I thought you were a Trump supporter. I'll never listen to your podcast again. In fact, I'm done with you."

All of this because I refused to embrace the violence and hatred and instead pointed to Jesus. Never mind I agreed with them that it was probable that millions of votes had been stolen. Never mind that I agreed with them that 74 million voters had been cheated. Never mind that I agreed with their suspicion that the mainstream media had carried Biden's water. They were angry because I stated my firm belief (which is fully supported by Scripture) that only one man is worthy of that kind of adoration and praise: Jesus Christ. I'm an American patriot, but that didn't matter. They railed against me because I took a stand on the fact that my true patriotism is with the only kingdom that can never be destroyed—the kingdom of the Son of God:

> In the time of those kings, the God of heaven will set up a kingdom that will never be destroyed. (Dan. 2:44)

I love America! But I'm standing, first and foremost, with God's kingdom on this one, and no one, from either the Right or the Left, will ever shake me on this. I pledge allegiance to the unshakable kingdom—always!

I Am Not in Despair

I am alarmed, but I am not in despair. My purpose in writing this book is to offer an alternative to the anger and chaos that are beginning to define who we are. I want to make the case that

America's greatest problem is not political but spiritual. I'll also argue that if our problem is spiritual, then the solution must be spiritual too. Rather than just attacking or supporting one -ism over another (socialism, capitalism, transgenderism, conservatism, liberalism, etc.), I want to reintroduce the Almighty back into our nation's public conversation since I'm confident that he alone is qualified to offer real solutions to what is tormenting us. There is a way out of this mess, but party politics and personal attacks are utterly useless in providing a pathway to national health because they rely on human reasoning. I'm not that smart, but I'm smart enough to know my limitations and the limitations of all of humanity in guiding our steps. Only God can do that.

I know this road will not be an easy one to travel because there are some people, for one reason or another, who just won't tolerate anyone who talks about America needing a supreme, almighty, and eternal God at the core of our national consciousness. I'm sure some will angrily gnash their teeth and froth at the mouth in response to what I am proposing. Remember this, though: I will make every attempt to center my argument in the Word of God and not write about my personal worldview. Instead, I have done what I can to give you the wisdom of God that is revealed in his Word. Don't take my word for it, however. Open your Bibles as you read along and fact-check me. I'm more than okay with that.

We have one shot at giving the greatest country in the history of the world another opportunity to repent and return to its spiritual roots. The way I figure it, if anyone wants to rise up in indignation and attack me, I can handle it because I'm just the messenger. I'm making a case for God, so they aren't really rejecting me at all. At the end of the day, I'll be looking for his approval, not anyone else's. If I have that, I don't really care what anyone says about me in response to my offering them the words of life.

CHAPTER 1

WHAT IS CANCEL CULTURE?

Since, then, we know what it is to fear
the Lord, we try to persuade others.
2 Corinthians 5:11

Cancel culture! What is that? To be honest with you, I had no clue what that meant the first time I heard it. But it didn't take me long to figure out I had been a victim of it long before it became a thing. And a thing it has become.

Simply put, cancel culture's goal is to embarrass, intimidate, or cause someone to lose something of value, such as a contract, a job, or corporate revenue, in order to force the target to change their behavior. This is the experience I described earlier when the media came after me to coerce me into retracting the Bible verse I quoted about homosexuality to the *GQ* reporter. When they tried to cancel me, it worked. Unfortunately for those who wanted me fired from *Duck Dynasty*, it only lasted about forty-eight hours or so. I never missed a beat. Others, sadly, are not so fortunate.

The attempt to silence people by canceling them is much more widespread and even more powerful today than it was then. An example of what I'm talking about is what happened to Drew Brees, the former quarterback of the New Orleans Saints. In early 2020, a reporter asked Brees's opinion of the players who kneeled during the playing of the national anthem. His response, which many considered patriotic, was that he would "never agree with anybody disrespecting the flag." Brees immediately came under attack. The cyberuniverse erupted in a frenzy of indignation from the mainstream media, other players, and social media's keyboard warriors. Brees caved a day later and offered the required apology.[1]

Author J. K. Rowling also had an encounter with cancel culture in June 2020. Devex posted an opinion piece with the headline "Creating a More Equal Post-COVID-19 World for People Who Menstruate." The writers were trying to bring attention to the dangers women in developing countries faced during the pandemic. I assume they were trying to be sensitive to transgender people, so they did not use the word "women" in their article, even though biological women are the only ones who menstruate. Rowling sarcastically replied to the opinion piece on Twitter: "'People who menstruate?' I'm sure there used to be a word for those people. Someone help me out. Wumben? Wimpund? Woomud?" Of course, she was pretending to search for the word *woman*.[2]

I don't want to spend a lot of time talking about whether Rowling made a legitimate point or not. The point I want to make is that, even though Rowling has a reputation for being liberal in her political and social views, she was not immune to cancellation. In her case, the backlash on Twitter was enormous, even vicious. While she did have a few supporters, others reacted with hysteria and outrage. One user responded, "Aren't you a children's writer? Your fixation with the genitalia of strangers is unsettling."[3] Another wrote, "Stop hating trans people you awful weirdo."[4] Many Twitter users unsympathetically informed Rowling, "I hate you."

The thing I find most disturbing about the attack on Rowling is that no one attempted to discuss the facts of her opinion. The cancel culture attacked her with the understanding "We don't discuss. We don't attempt to persuade! We destroy! That's what we do!" I have a news flash for these people: simply telling folks to shut up doesn't really change any minds. Cancel culture may be effective at forcing people into submission, but it does nothing to persuade. In my humble opinion, people who respond with vulgarity (some of the responses to her tweet are too vulgar for me to repeat) and personal attacks indicate they aren't all that comfortable in their position. From where I sit, it looks as if they are afraid their point of view won't stand up to scrutiny.

Another celebrity who's taken it on the chin in recent years for allegedly going against the grain of the political and moral views of popular culture is the actor Chris Pratt. In spite of the fact that Pratt has never spoken publicly about his political views, Twitter users went after him when he didn't participate in a fundraiser for Joe Biden that was sponsored by his fellow Avengers actors. Some in Twitterland surmised, since he was absent from the event, he must be a Donald Trump supporter. Then he was attacked for attending what was described by his detractors as an "anti-LGBTQ" church, even though no one provided much evidence that it was true. When a Twitter poll was taken, where users were given the opportunity to eliminate one actor out of four named Chris, Pratt was the loser.[5]

Targeting celebrities for cancellation is one thing. Most of them can withstand any financial and professional hits their careers might take from the cancel culture. But what happens when this enraged crowd goes after regular folks? You know, people who work regular jobs for a living and often live paycheck to paycheck.

At the peak of the riots and unrest in the summer of 2020, a friend of a friend (I'll call him Bernard) was communicating on Facebook with a colleague who worked for the same nationally known corporation as he did. Bernard's colleague was sitting in her hotel room on the tenth floor and watching the violence unfold on the streets below in a midwestern city where she was attending a conference. The rioters were breaking windows, entering private businesses, and attempting to breach the front door of the hotel that Bernard's friend was staying in. She posted a few pictures of the violence on her thread and commented that police snipers were stationed atop other buildings with rifles that fired rubber bullets. Bernard replied the police should direct a few rubber bullets toward the violent protesters and disperse the crowd because of the danger posed to the public.

Within a single hour both Bernard and his colleague were notified by their corporation's lawyers that their employment had been immediately terminated for their "insensitive" posts on social media.

Boom! In one hour, they had lost it all. Fired! Canceled!

Jack Phillips is an ordinary businessman who owns the Masterpiece Cakeshop in Lakewood, Colorado. But in 2012 he was thrust into the national spotlight in a way he never anticipated. A same-sex couple had wanted to hire Phillips to bake a wedding cake for their upcoming nuptials. When he refused to make a cake that celebrated a wedding he felt went against his religious beliefs, the couple sued him in court. Eventually, the case wound up in the Supreme Court, where the justices determined Jack was within his rights to refuse the couple's request.

One would think the radical LGBTQ community would get the message and simply leave the humble baker alone. If you thought that, you would be wrong. In 2017, on the day the Supreme Court agreed to hear Jack's case, he received a call from a customer who wanted a cake that would be blue on the outside and pink on the inside to celebrate the caller's transition from male to female. Once again Jack refused.

As I said, the state of Colorado and the LGBTQ community should have received a very clear message from their earlier inter-action with the baker, but they didn't. Now he's back in court defending his right to not promote anything he feels is against his beliefs.[6]

This is cancel culture. No free exchange of ideas. No respectful back-and-forth to arrive at a consensus. Just rip open your laptop or your iPhone and attack. Intimidate! Destroy! Overwhelm your opponents and bring them to their knees. Drew Brees and J. K. Rowling were punished for violating someone else's sensibilities. They said what these people did not want to hear. But they are wealthy celebrities, and they'll survive.

But what about Bernard and his colleague? What about Jack the baker? They aren't high-profile people. They are just hard-working folks trying to provide a decent life for their families. Yet they were canceled, too, and for them it was very costly. And for what? Did they commit acts of treason against the United States? Were they guilty of thievery? Had they sexually harassed their coworkers? Were they dealing drugs? No, it was nothing like that.

The sad truth is that, in the cases of Jack Phillips and Bernard and his colleague, the price they paid for stating their beliefs may have been more costly than the price I paid for quoting a Bible verse. I lost a few sponsorships; they lost their ability to make a living.

In the case of Bernard, the corporation he and his friend worked for failed to defend both common sense and freedom of speech. You may be wondering why the company caved so quickly and fired them. I'm not sure, but maybe the reason is that the corporation was afraid the players within the cancel culture would publicly shame the company for tolerating *offensive* and *hurtful* speech within their corporation. Until then, Bernard and his friend had both been top producers in the company. Now, they were out on the streets for one crime: they had exercised their First Amendment rights and violated an unknown and unwritten company policy. The cancel culture crowd won when the company caved. Unfortunately, Bernard and his coworker were caught in the middle.

Perhaps you are wondering who these cancel culture warriors are. In the case of Bernard, the person who canceled him and his friend later posted on social media that he spends a great deal of his "workday" searching for "offensive" posts. His goal is to expose as many regular people's "transgressions" as he can and publicly shame them. Apparently, there is a small army of folks like him who troll the cyberuniverse to do just what this young man did: to get people canceled. In my opinion, this is a miserable way to live, to spend your life looking through social media posts for something, for someone you can destroy. How sad!

Before we go any further, I think it's important to point out it's not just people on the Left who are canceling others out. Some evangelical Christians are pretty good at doing it too. In 2008, Rick Warren, the pastor of the California megachurch Saddleback, hosted the Civil Forum on the Presidency between the two presidential candidates, Barack Obama and John McCain. Later, Obama asked Warren to deliver the prayer at his inauguration. Of course, many on the left side of the cultural spectrum attacked Obama's choice of Warren to deliver the prayer, but many Christians also went after Warren for his association with Obama's inauguration.

I'll admit I'm not the most subtle man to ever live, nor am I all that familiar with thinking about the optics of a move such as Warren made. But the way I figure it, even if Bubba asks me to pray at closing time at the local redneck juke joint, I'll jump at the chance. What better opportunity to go before the Father and proclaim his name in the presence of the people who need him more than they know? Perhaps the evangelical naysayers hadn't considered the opportunity that Warren's prayer in front of the nation presented before they attempted to cancel him.

Shades of Cancel Culture in Christians

I want you to contrast how cancel culture tries to coerce folks to submit to an agenda with how mature believers attempt to spread their message. Paul wrote in 2 Corinthians 5:11, "Since, then, we know what it is to fear the Lord, we try to *persuade* others" (emphasis added). In my younger days as a Christian, my goal was to back people into a corner and intimidate them into baptism. As I grew in maturity, though, I realized the real power is in the message, not the messenger. Coercive or heavy-handed preaching may have resulted in a boatload of conversions, but I had misunderstood my role in leading others to Jesus.

Today? Well, I'm still very passionate about speaking the name of Jesus into the hearts and minds of people who are messed up in the same way I once was. Now, however, I am more about persuading. I want to make an appeal that gives people an opportunity to change their minds about the direction of their lives. I want them to make up their own minds and approach God with the full confidence that he will accept them and that he loved them while they were still enemies with him (Rom. 5:6–8). I want them to be fully persuaded that the sacrifice of Christ is all the proof they'll ever need to know how much he loves them. But no matter how passionate I am about others putting on Christ, I decided years ago I would not use coercion and intimidation to "get people in the water." I guess you could say I abandoned cancel culture tactics long before cancel culture became known as cancel culture.

I also decided years ago that I would handle disagreements the way God told me to handle them. Jesus said, "If your brother or sister sins, go and point out their fault, just between the two of you. If they listen to you, you have won them over" (Matt. 18:15). You may think I'm a bit naive here, but the way I figure it, the simplest approach is to handle it in God's way. I never go wrong when I listen to the Spirit of God. I've noticed that people who do the opposite of what Jesus said in this passage have a cloud of chaos and disorder trailing behind them everywhere they go. We've always had people who take their disagreements to the streets and announce them publicly, and usually they were trying to cancel another person, to convince others to side with them and shun the person with whom they disagree.

As I said earlier, it's not just people of the world who publicly attack their opponents. In the months leading up to the 2021 Southern Baptist Convention, Twitter and other social media platforms erupted with Baptists attacking one another over issues such as critical race theory, women preaching, sexual abuse cover-ups, and social justice issues. I wondered at the time what would have happened if the parties involved had first obeyed Matthew 18:15. I'm assuming some of those involved had already attempted to sit down with one another and open the Book and pray for God's guidance. But I suspect few of them did, judging by their language in the exchanges.

I don't want to repeat their comments here, but many were reproduced in a June 12, 2021, *Washington Post* article titled "Secret Recordings, Leaked Letters: Explosive Secrets Rocking the Southern Baptist Convention."[7] I'm not in the inner circle of the Southern Baptist Convention, but this sounds more like Washington, DC, than it does the representatives of the bride of Christ, the church of God. The article quoted several prominent church leaders who had publicly blasted one another on a variety of issues. Publicly! Jesus followers ripping one another publicly to cancel the influence of the other. I'm just an average man, but I am certain Christ is not glorified in this. Not even a little bit.

I'm saddened by all of this, but I'm not shocked. I wasn't around in the first century, but from what I've read in the New Testament and from what I've observed about human nature, attempting to cancel others is as old as the hills, even among Christians. This is what Paul was referring to in Philippians 1:15–17: "It is true that some preach Christ out of envy and rivalry, but others out of goodwill. The latter do so out of love, knowing that I am put here for the defense of the gospel. The former preach Christ out of selfish ambition, not sincerely, supposing that they can stir up trouble for me while I am in chains." Those who were attacking him also preached Jesus, but they were perverting the message of the gospel in an effort to neutralize Paul's influence.

Of course, the ultimate attempt to cancel was how the power brokers in the Jewish religious institution orchestrated the murder of Christ. They were religious leaders too. When the chief priests and the Sanhedrin stirred up the hastily assembled crowd, they began to parade a slew of witnesses to bring a string of false accusations against the Lord. When nothing worked, they said, "We heard him say, 'I will destroy this temple *made with human hands* and in three days will build another, not made with hands'" (Mark 14:58, emphasis added).

You may not be familiar with this tactic of the chief priests, but it's an old one. Take a little truth and tweak it a bit to make your accusation stick. In this case, Jesus had said, "Destroy this temple, and I will raise it again in three days" (John 2:19). The problem is, he wasn't referring to Solomon's temple but to his body, foretelling his resurrection from the grave. They simply added the words "made with human hands," which made it sound as if Jesus had said something he neither said nor meant to say.

There was no social media in the first century, but that didn't prevent the cancel culture from doing its thing. Unfortunately, people now have the platform of social media, which makes their gossip and slander much more dangerous because it's so much easier to execute. Gossip and half-truths can travel around the globe in less than a second. It must have taken the Jewish leaders a couple of hours to assemble their crowd; now it could be done almost instantaneously.

Make no mistake about it, intimidation and the fear of cancellation is a powerful strategy. The average American is walking on eggshells, trying to avoid breaking the cardinal rule of the cancel culture religion: *Be kind! Don't offend! Don't judge! Tolerate!*

Maybe you are wondering, what's wrong with that? These are attributes we should all strive for, right? They are, after all, the "fruit of the Spirit." I agree. I strive to be kind, but cancel culture is not actually interested in *all of us* being kind, loving, and nonjudgmental. If you don't believe me, just break a rule. One time. Just violate their mandate and speak out against something they want to promote. You will find they themselves are not all that committed to kindness. Ask J. K. Rowling and Drew Brees. Ask Bernard and Jack Phillips.

Even though the rule is to be kind, loving, and nonjudgmental, it doesn't always apply because there is a hidden exception to the rule: you are permitted to be unloving, unkind, and judgmental if you are calling out someone *you* decide isn't loving, kind, and nonjudgmental. Then you can hate and judge all you want to. But other than that, there are no exceptions.

Some people who participate in cancel culture probably believe they're engaging in discussion and may also believe they are directed by God to share their opinion. But I've noticed we rarely find ourselves engaged in a free exchange of ideas. That's because what cancel culture is really after is a good old-fashioned beatdown of anyone who crosses the line. It's about emotional manipulation that is designed to force people into submission. In the dangerous game of cancel culture, there are no winners because no one ever knows what the real rules are. No one knows what can be offensive or not. For example, I'm told that kids have been playing with Mr. Potato Head since it first came to the toy stores in 1952. But in 2020 critics began to argue that the gender-specific Mr. Potato Head reinforced hurtful gender stereotypes and could cause children who identified as nontraditional genders to feel left out. So Hasbro, the company that owns Mr. Potato Head, made the "bold" decision to remove the "Mr." from all future packaging, and Mr. Potato Head would hereafter be known as simply Potato Head. I guess transitioning from one gender to another or to no gender at all is now mainstream. Even Mr. Potato Head is doing it. I'm sure we are all better off, right?

The problem with this shifting cultural landscape is that none of us ever knows what the next offensive trigger point might be. One day it was Mr. Potato Head, and the next it was Dr. Seuss perpetuating hurtful stereotypes. I'm just a simple guy, but even I can figure out that nothing good will come of this. One day Mr. Potato Head is a funny toy that allows kids to be creative by changing his appearance, and the next day he is a symbol of everything that is wrong in America. I'm pretty sure that no kid ever said to himself, "This toy offends me and causes me to feel marginalized."

The story here is that you can be innocent one day only to be guilty of the most heinous cultural offense the next. In a world like that, you never know where you stand. No one can live up to that standard. No one. Not even the people who participate in cancel culture can.

Let me give you an example of this. In 2021, celebrity Chrissy Teigen shared a lengthy apology for publicly shaming and canceling other celebrities. I read her apology, and I think she seems sincere enough. In my world, when someone tells me they are sorry for wronging me, I'm like, "Hey, it's no big deal." In fact, I make it a practice to forgive folks before they ask. That way I'm not walking through life carrying a boatload of hurt feelings. But fashion designer Michael Costello responded in a since-deleted Instagram post that Teigen's bullying had caused him years of grief: "For the past 7 years, I've lived with a deep unhealed trauma. I wanted to kill myself and I am still traumatized, depressed and have thoughts of suicide."[8]

But hold on a second! As soon as Costello published his response, singer Leona Lewis claimed that Costello had body-shamed her at a 2014 charity event. Did you get that? Costello claimed that Teigen hurt his feelings with her cyberbullying, and then Lewis claimed Costello had hurt her feelings in 2014.[9]

I'll admit I'm not someone who wears my feelings on my sleeve, so all of this drama is foreign to me. But the point I want to make is that once we go down the road of calling others out in public while demanding fair treatment for ourselves, we are going to wind up in hot water for being guilty of the same thing. Guilty party number one calls out guilty party number two for causing public shame only to have guilty party number three remind guilty party number two that he or she is guilty of the same thing. If your head is spinning, join the crowd. This isn't a sustainable way to live. Everyone winds up getting burned because everyone falls short—all of us are guilty of saying things we shouldn't say or being insensitive to the feelings of others.

Is any of this fair? Well, no, it isn't. But I don't want to waste a lot of time thinking about what is fair. If we are going to wait until things are fair, we will be a very frustrated group of individuals. I choose to forgo the right to have things fair. Besides, if I demand fairness, then God would do the fair thing: he would destroy me for my crime of rebellion against him. Instead of fairness, I'm far more concerned about making sure I introduce God into my interactions with folks who practice cancel culture. And I want to do that in a way that accurately reflects who he really is. That's why I wrote this book; I want to give a biblical view of Christ. My goal is to convince you and others (including the PC cancel culture crowd) that the only way anyone is going to find meaning and fulfillment in life is to seek the God who is real, to pursue the one who died for us and was raised from the dead on our behalf. Instead of political correctness, I'm all about biblical correctness. That's the only thing that concerns me, because at the end of the day, I'll not stand before you or any other person to account for how I lived my life. No, I will only stand before the Almighty, because he alone has the right and the authority to hold me accountable. The same is true for you. So getting fair treatment from other people is the last thing on my mind. I seek to please the one who is infinitely fair. Thankfully, he is full of grace, mercy, and forgiveness.

My goal, and I would suggest you think about making it yours too, is not to destroy the people in the cancel culture movement. That job is way above my pay grade. Instead, I'm focused on one thing: I want to understand what this crowd is up to because I want to be ready to "give an answer to everyone who asks you to give the reason for the hope that you have" (1 Peter 3:15). I understand that this bunch has experienced an adrenaline rush of power, and their next step will be to grab a little more. But I do not want to respond in the same way they do, with anger, hatred, bitterness, and control. I'm not out to destroy them just because I disagree with them. I want to have a meaningful, respectful conversation with them instead. I want to persuade them that God is real and that we can trust him.

While it's true I detest the practices of cancel culture, as a follower of Christ, I have to be careful that I am not guilty of doing what they do. I don't want to treat them the same way they treat me. I want to do things the way God has instructed me to do them. That's because I want to be obedient to God, not cause anyone to slander his name because of me. Since I'm committed to being as Christlike as possible (because of what he's done for me), I am also committed to running my response to cancel culture through the only reliable filter I know. I want to make sure that I'm handling it *his* way, and this is how he said to respond to opposition:

> And the Lord's servant must not be quarrelsome but must be kind to everyone, able to teach, not resentful. Opponents must be gently instructed, in the hope that God will grant them repentance leading them to a knowledge of the truth, and that they will come to their senses and escape from the trap of the devil, who has taken them captive to do his will. (2 Tim. 2:24–28)

Cancel culture is not about a specific person or even a group of people; it's an idea that caught a stiff breeze and was fanned into flames by people who are confused about what is right and good. And why wouldn't they be? I'll repeatedly make the point that without a firm faith in a transcendent God, who alone has the authority to determine what is right, we are basically on our own.

Without God, we are adrift on the sea of life without any sense of direction. Yes, *confusion* is the word I would use to describe the minds of those who don't know God. As a matter of fact, I remember the confused life I lived before the Almighty got hold of me. And if there's one thing I know about confused people, it's that they have no idea there is a God who offers to give their minds clarity. God is not the source of confusion (1 Cor. 14:33), but there is one who does love confusion: the "father of lies," the Evil One (John 8:44). He loves to muddy the waters. He loves to muddle our minds with bad ideas and half-truths. That's why I'm not into attacking those who attack me. I am much more interested in attacking the ideas that confuse us than I am in attacking any person or group of people. As you can see in the verse above, treating our opponents with kindness and respect is a very biblical idea. This is why I make every attempt to *gently* instruct folks; since I'm working for the Almighty, I also want them to come to their senses and escape the trap of the devil, just as I did.

Trust me when I tell you I understand the temptation to respond by attacking this crowd. I am certainly not saying my track record is perfect on this, but the gentle instructive response is my goal because that is how the Almighty has instructed me to respond. I'm pretty sure he knows more about the best way to react than I.

Yes, it's a war zone out there for sure, but our opponents are not actually the media nor cancel culture nor the radical Left nor the radical Right. In fact, our opposition is not a person at all. Satan is definitely our enemy. We are at war with *his* deadly ideas that have established a stronghold in the minds of unsuspecting and ignorant people. In response to that, we are firing our spiritual AR-15s at arguments that distort the reality about God and other people.

People don't get killed in the war that God has called us to fight, at least not by us. Rather, we are all about freeing them from the lies that distort minds and destroy lives. We aren't a plundering, murdering horde engaged in a relentless battle to bring a gruesome, bloody war into the streets. Other people may wage war with the intention of destroying others, but not us. Instead, we are liberators because our goal is to bring freedom in Christ, freedom from deadly thoughts that stand in opposition to the knowledge of God. Yes, we fight, but we don't fight as they fight:

> The weapons we fight with are not the weapons of the world. On the contrary, they have divine power to demolish strong-holds. We demolish arguments and every pretension that sets itself up against the knowledge of God, and we take captive every thought to make it obedient to Christ. (2 Cor. 10:4–5)

Do you see the difference? One person battles against personalities, but the wise and godly person wages war against falsehoods because those ideas will end badly for anyone who embraces them. One destroys people while the other seeks to destroy destructive thinking that is not rooted in reality. Rather than forcing people to submit to us by exercising our raw power, we are persuading people to embrace freedom from bondage.

At this point, you might ask, "Phil, how would we know which ideas need to be attacked and destroyed?"

I would say, based on the passage above, that a bad idea is one that sets itself up against the truth about God. Any idea that leads us to put our hope and trust in anything other than the gospel of Christ must be attacked. Any idea that deceives people with false hope and leads to bondage has to go.

I want to encourage you to fight the good fight against the real enemy! Don't get confused about who that is. Identify your opponent and fight him relentlessly! Fight using the weapons God has given you, and fight with passion! You may be canceled in the process, but don't worry, it's only temporary. In the meantime, you are in possession of the one thing that will last forever—immortality! No one can cancel that.

CHAPTER 2

WHERE DID CANCEL CULTURE COME FROM?

Furthermore, just as they did not think it
worthwhile to retain the knowledge of God,
so God gave them over to a depraved mind, so
that they do what ought not to be done.
Romans 1:28

I'm not into social media very much. In fact, I don't even own a computer or a cell phone. I've never even turned one on. When I tell people that, they smirk as if I'm some kind of caveman. But I'm comfortable with the fact that it is almost impossible to draw me into cancel culture wars that are played out on the internet, because I'm not on it.

Social media seems to have helped cancel culture take on a life of its own over the past few years. I suppose when a deeply divided country is addicted to social media, this is what we get. Now everyone has a platform to anonymously comment on any topic they choose without actually being responsible for the damage they do.

Still, I sense there is more at play in twenty-first-century America than simply the advent of social media. From where I sit, I see a much more sinister mood sweeping over the nation. As I've observed human behavior changing and becoming more violent and combative over the past forty-five years or so, I've often wondered, what's really going on? Is there an unseen master plan to fundamentally move us away from the principles our founders laid down that made us the greatest nation in the history of the world?

The sad answer is yes, there is a master plan to transform America from the core that made it a bastion of freedom and prosperity. There is a growing crowd who would have us become more like the godless communist countries that have ruled large chunks of the world's population for most of the past hundred years or so.

Cancel culture isn't the disease; it's a symptom of this shift in how more and more Americans are defining what our republic should look like. I don't know when the change began, but I remember when I first began to hear the term *political correctness* being tossed around. Political correctness is the practice of avoiding words that others might consider offensive. The result is that, over the years, we found ourselves using new words to describe old ideas. For example, when more women began to enter the workforce, we stopped saying that someone was a fireman or a salesman and began to refer to them as firefighters and sales professionals. I'm old enough to remember when older unmarried women were known as spinsters or old maids. Now the politically correct term would be unmarried women.

All of this is innocent enough, but as with all good ideas, political correctness (PC) has gotten out of hand. Take what the Beano did to Dennis the Menace, as an example. They reworked the Dennis character to make him less of a menace and rebranded him as simply Dennis.[1] Maybe they should have marketed him as Dennis the Very Nice Boy! If you ask me, that sounds like a show that would put me to sleep, a very deep sleep. But at least it is politically correct.

Or how about this insane example of PC speech. According to the BBC News Channel, an executive with a job search agency in Hertfordshire, England, was told she could not use the terms *reliable* or *hardworking* when advertising for workers because the terms might be offensive to unreliable people.[2] Crazy, huh? What would a job agency's purpose be other than to find hardworking and reliable employees for people to hire? I wonder how that works when she calls her client and says, "I have a worker for you who is immediately available. But I'm not sure she is hardworking and reliable." I'm sure that'll work, right?

PC, in a very real sense, was the mother of cancel culture. It is the movement that trained us to be sensitive to even the most irrational and outrageous demands of people who are easily offended. All political correctness needed to spawn the cancel culture movement was to find a breeding partner, and she found it in social media. Unfortunately for America, this union that produced cancel culture is chipping away at the core of what makes us a great nation.

Our founders envisioned a much different union. It's probably been a while since you've read the preamble to the US Constitution, so I'll offer it here:

> We the People of the United States, in Order to form a more perfect Union, establish Justice, insure domestic Tranquility, provide for the common defence, promote the general Welfare, and secure the Blessings of Liberty to ourselves and our Posterity, do ordain and establish this Constitution for the United States of America.[3]

Why were we different from Communist countries such as the old Soviet Union and China? What distinguished us from France, Great Britain, and Germany in the 1700s? Why was yesterday's America different from the America of today? The difference is that the goal of our founders was to establish a more perfect union, not a perfect union, but one that was progressively more perfect. It would be a union that would seek to promote the blessings of liberty for posterity and encourage the general welfare of its citizens. It would be a union whose goal was justice for all. It wasn't a union forged on pettiness and party politics but rather the idea that all of us were created equal by nature's God.

I'm afraid contemporary America is incapable of producing a document anything like the Constitution because our culture is infatuated with instant gratification. We can't wait for an imperfect union to become more perfect. We want it now. Right *now*! We demand it, and if it doesn't happen immediately, we are taking our case to the streets!

I don't know of a claim by any of our founders that the new nation would be perfectly free of injustice or that we would enjoy perfect domestic tranquility. But I will point out these qualities were their goal. Most of our founders possessed an inner voice and a deep conviction that God is real and that we were created by him to enjoy liberated lives in fellowship with him.

You may be interested to know this is what drives me too. Every day, from the time I arise in the morning until the time I lay down at night, one stream of thought drives everything I do. It's a simple message, really. It's the theme of my life that serves as my road map. As I go about my daily business, I am continually aware of a few very important facts. These facts shape my view of life, my worldview—and every word, thought, and action has to pass my worldview test.

As I said, it is a simple test, but it sure isn't easy to make certain my life conforms to what God has told me about life and reality. For one thing, I know the only way to explain my own existence is that everything was created by an all-powerful, kind, benevolent God. That's the only reason I am here. Second, I am well aware of the fact I rebelled against him and went my own way. But I'm also continually aware of the fact that this God I serve rescued me from the eternal consequences of my rebellion against him by sending his Son to die in my stead. I also know he raised Jesus from the grave and took him to sit at his right hand until he sends him back to take us to where the Father is.

That's it! These facts are the foundation of my life. Actually, my foundation is a person: Jesus Christ. But it's the facts I know about him that motivate me. As it turns out, these facts are also the foundation of our republic. This story says we all matter because God created us in his image. We matter because God says we do. This is not to say we are better than others but that God is better. Those of us who follow Christ aren't superior, we just follow a superior being. This is important because knowing these things about God and about ourselves eliminates chaos and confusion. We don't have to wonder if the path we are on is the correct one when we follow him. We know he's certain about where to go and how to get there, so we tag along behind him.

So what is the other side after? What drives them? I can tell you this: they are not motivated by faith in the God of the Bible. I am desperate for them to follow him, but at this point many do not. He's absent from their worldview, and that fact alone produces an entirely different vision for America. And any vision for our nation that does not include God produces a very different outcome. It produces the America you are beginning to see. Angry, violent, judgmental, and ready to cancel.

We'll come back to this point later, but if you're wondering what the difference is between the two competing philosophies that are at work in America, this is it. People like me recognize that we are too weak to direct our own steps, so we turn to God for help. The other side believes that we can redeem ourselves, that we can make ourselves better just by trying harder, by doing better.

Can Man Perfect Himself?

In June 1962, dozens of so-called student radicals occupied a retreat center owned by the United Auto Workers in Port Huron, Michigan. Their purpose was to draft a new manifesto for the offspring of the Greatest Generation (the children of the men and women who defeated Nazi Germany and Imperial Japan). This new manifesto would be a statement that would serve as the blueprint for how they would change the world and would give these radicals tremendous power and authority over the next few decades.[4]

Chances are you've never even heard of *The Port Huron Statement*. And if you are younger than sixty years old, you've probably never heard of the Students for a Democratic Society (SDS) either, but you might want to familiarize yourself with them and their agenda because the America you see today is living out the SDS philosophy. The angry radical crowds on both sides of the spectrum exist today because the student radicals of the early sixties set out to change America's foundational principles, and their agenda began to resonate with people.

I read *The Port Huron Statement*, and one thought popped into my mind as I neared the end of the document. *There's no God in this!* Can you believe it? It's not that I'm at odds with them over the need to correct injustices. Neither is the Almighty. God is a God of justice, and when people are unjust, he takes a very dim view of that too:

Do not deny justice to your poor people in their lawsuits.
(Ex. 23:6)

WHERE DID CANCEL CULTURE COME FROM?

Do not deprive the foreigner or the fatherless of justice, or
    take the cloak of the widow as a pledge. (Deut. 24:17)
For the LORD is righteous, he loves justice; the upright will
    see his face. (Ps. 11:7)

One thing the SDS agreed with God about is that no one can prosper without justice. These students weren't wrong to point out that injustice anywhere threatens the dignity of every person everywhere. But their mistake was assuming we could simply pull ourselves up out of the mire of an unjust war and racism by our bootstraps. That we could just do it on our own, by sheer determination and will. It didn't work. The Vietnam War is over now, but racism is as big a topic in America as it ever was. Maybe bigger.

The SDS was plain about what they thought would bring about real change in America, and it unfortunately did not involve the Almighty:

We regard men as infinitely precious and possessed of unfulfilled capacities for reason, freedom, and love. In affirming these principles we are aware of countering perhaps the dominant conceptions of man in the twentieth century: that he is a thing to be manipulated, and that he is inherently incapable of directing his own affairs. . . .

Men have unrealized potential for self-cultivation, self-direction, self-understanding, and creativity. It is this potential that we regard as crucial and to which we appeal, not to the human potentiality for violence, unreason, and submission to authority.[5]

Maybe you live on the Snake River in Idaho or you have a cabin in the Upper Peninsula of Michigan. Maybe you hunt and fish. You probably beat the sun up every day and work hard to provide for your family. We all live life a little differently, but most of us have one thing in common: we live in the world of common sense. So let me ask you this, What does that even mean? Self-cultivation? Self-direction? Self-understanding? Creativity? Directing his own affairs?

The SDS founders may have had good intentions, but it didn't take long for things to go sour with them. The group splintered into factions, including groups with names such as the Weathermen or the Weather Underground. This group, along with some of the other splinter groups, was radicalized even further and began to employ terrorist tactics, including the bombing of police stations, the US Capitol, and the Pentagon. In 2001, founding member Bill Ayers told *New York Times* reporter Dinitia Smith, "I don't regret setting the bombs. . . . I feel we didn't do enough." When she asked him if he would do it again, he replied, "I don't want to discount the possibility."[6]

I mention this only because it points out that fighting injustice without an overarching view that God is ultimately in control ends up frustrating activists such as Ayers. If you are truly committed to a cause, as Ayers obviously was, it's easy to understand how one's patience with culture would wear thin and you would feel compelled to take matters into your own hands. If a cause relies solely on humanistic reasoning and power, then one of two things must happen. Either the movement will fizzle away as its members grow increasingly frustrated at the slow pace of change or it must ramp up the rhetoric and take action and try to force an outcome. Sadly, the only result of violence and anger is more violence and anger. Nothing really gets better. Things only get worse. Without God to temper our outrage, our anger can become more important than the things we say we are angry about. Rage becomes the god of the godless.

This is exactly what we find in Scripture:

> Why do the nations rage
> > and the peoples plot in vain?
> The kings of the earth set themselves,
> > and the rulers take counsel together,
> > > against the LORD and against his Anointed,
> > > > saying,
> "Let us burst their bonds apart
> > and cast away their cords from us." (Ps.
> > > 2:1–3 ESV)

Where does the rage come from? It comes from throwing off God's restraints and setting ourselves up as the ultimate rulers. Sadly, God put those restraints in place to protect us and guide us to a life that is fulfilling and meaningful, not to deprive us.

I don't know when the shift away from God began, but I can tell you the root of everything that ails us can be found in the values section of *The Port Huron Statement*. One single word tells us all we need to know about what caused us to get off track: *self.* The SDS didn't cause America to fall away from God; they were only reflecting the cancer that was already lurking in America's soul. God was already in the process of being expelled. But even though they didn't cause America's exodus from its godly roots, they certainly made a clear argument for the idea that we can elevate ourselves without God. No God, just human reasoning. Self!

"So what's wrong with that?" you might ask. "Don't you believe in self-cultivation, self-understanding, self-direction, and creativity, Phil?" If you posed that question to me, I would tell you that I'd love to believe in our ability to self-direct. I really would. But Houston, we have a problem. So far we have not proven that we are able to self-direct. I see no evidence that we have demonstrated "unfulfilled capacities for reason, freedom, and love." So far, all I've seen is that we are capable of unspeakable horrors when we are on our own.

If you think I'm wrong, just think about it. What do you say about our ability to be good on our own? Do you think we've been successful at self-cultivation, self-direction, self-understanding, and creativity? When you look at our track record over the past five thousand years, do you see goodness? Do you see humanity improving? Or do you see humanity becoming more inhumane, more self-destructive, rising up and killing other human beings by the millions?

As evidence of what I'm talking about, think about every political system you've ever heard of that engaged in ethnic cleansing, political executions, and arbitrary imprisonments. They all have one thing in common: there's no God in their political philosophy. Pol Pot killed two million people in only four years, which accounted for one-fourth of Cambodia's population. The brutal Soviet dictator Joseph Stalin killed an estimated twenty million people in thirty years. Adolf Hitler? He exterminated two-thirds of Europe's Jewish population, some six million human beings.

And what did these three murderers have in common? They tried to change their national culture without God.

A biblical example of someone who rejected the Word of God and took matters into his own hands is the Israelite king Saul (1 Sam. 15). God had specifically commanded him to destroy the Amalekites for an unprovoked attack on the Israelites as they were coming out of Egypt. And Saul almost obeyed God. Almost.

But not quite. He slaughtered them all—except for the livestock and the Amalekite king, Agag. I suppose he wanted to parade him through the towns of Israel as a trophy, signifying his prowess as a military leader. Whatever his motives were, his refusal to obey God because of his reliance on his own flawed human understanding resulted in severe consequences for Saul and his sons; they were all killed in battle. And God placed David on Saul's throne.

Here's the way I figure it: if the God of the Bible is real, then I can bank everything I have on him being truthful and reliable. I don't have to second-guess him at all. In fact, every time I've tried that, it hasn't worked out for me. But besides my own personal experience with self-reliance, I see the evidence in the historical record. It never works out well for any individual or nation when they evict God and his wisdom from their minds and hearts.

In spite of our clear failure to achieve goodness by following our own minds and hearts, *The Port Huron Statement* writers declared that we should run from "submission to authority."[7] My question is this: How does that work out for us if we cast off authority? Just look at that word for a moment. The root word for authority is *author*, as in a person who writes text. If I were to write a book explaining the intricacies of brain surgery, for example, I would suggest you pay no attention to anything I say on the subject. In fact, if you see some redneck holding my book on brain surgery in one hand and a scalpel in the other hand, well, all I can say is you'd better run for your life. But if I penned a book titled *The Expert Guide to Duck Hunting*, you can pretty much depend on every word I write. As the author of a book like that, I would be an authority. That's one subject I know something about.

Here's what I would say to the authors of *The Port Huron*

Statement: Run from submission to authority? You must be confused! I'm running *toward* submission to authority. And here's why. In Acts 3, Peter and John had just healed a man born with a disability. When the people ran to the place where the healing occurred, Peter told the crowd about the only reliable authority, the Author of Life:

> The God of Abraham, Isaac and Jacob, the God of our fathers, has glorified his servant Jesus. You handed him over to be killed, and you disowned him before Pilate, though he had decided to let him go. You disowned the Holy and Righteous One and asked that a murderer be released to you. You killed the author of life, but God raised him from the dead. (vv. 13–15)

Run from authority? Not me! The last thing I want to do is try to live on my own. The fact is, I need authority if I am going to live out my days here on planet Earth with any kind of meaning and purpose. I sure can't just pull purpose out of thin air. Instead, I must have authority for the choices I make for how I am going to live my life. The truth is, we all make this choice. Either we throw off the authority of the one who not only created us but also died and was raised from the dead for us or we trust him and submit to him. Either we choose to live our lives by the authority of human wisdom and reason or we put our faith in God's wisdom. Before you decide which you will choose, I beg you to consider the track record of each point of view.

From where I sit, I don't think America is better off since it began to abandon submission to God. If you ignore the authority of God when you lay out your path, you have only one choice: you are on your own. This was the flaw of the SDS statement and all human constructs that ignore God. But I would argue that, by all indications, we are worse off, much worse off. If the goal of the SDS was to make America a better place, they missed the mark. Is America good today? Or do you see what I see: more violence in the streets, more homelessness, more opioid addiction, more aborted children. Rather than inching toward goodness, we are sliding into depravity, anger, malice, slander, and hatred. Nope! We are far worse today than we were only a couple of generations ago.

Take what has happened to our families since we severed ties to the spiritual principles upon which our republic rested in the beginning. I'm sure they weren't connected events, but at about the same time *The Port Huron Statement* was published, state governments all across the country began to dismantle the nuclear family by making divorce much easier. Until the 1960s, divorce was rare by today's standards. In 1960, the divorce rate was 2.2 per thousand Americans.[8] By 2000, the number had risen to 8.2 per thousand.[9]

But even these numbers don't tell the whole story. As if the exploding divorce statistics weren't bad enough, the increasing number of babies born to single moms began to grow even faster. In 1960, the percentage of births to unmarried women hovered in the single digits.[10] As of 2019, the number of women giving birth without being married has skyrocketed to 40 percent.[11]

While I applaud any woman who has the task of raising her children by herself, the impact on society of so many fatherless children has been devastating. Children raised without fathers are far more likely to live in poverty their entire lives, find themselves in trouble with the law more often, and will themselves be more likely to give birth to children out of wedlock.

When we cast off authority and use our own wisdom and understanding to craft our own plan for how we should live as individuals and as a society, this is the kind of chaos that follows. The cultural and sexual revolutions of the 1960s promised liberation from the authority of God without any consequences. The only problem is, they failed to deliver. We are now living in a culture that is growing in its disdain for the authority of God, or anyone else for that matter, and the negative impact on our country is profound.

Yes, the cultural revolutionaries of the 1960s promised an imminent utopia, but after sixty years, we aren't living in a utopia by anyone's estimation. Millions of children from broken and dysfunctional families grow into adulthood without any real sense of direction, and that creates an environment ripe for something such as cancel culture. How would anyone know how to find a way to a meaningful life once any real discussion about the reality of God and his love for us has been eliminated from all public discussion? Without an earthly father and certainly without a heavenly Father, we wouldn't know how to treat our neighbors. How would we know to work hard and contribute to society in positive ways? We wouldn't know, and that's a problem. When we have no road map other than our own wisdom, we don't know where to turn, so we turn on one another. We attack one another for our ethnicities and our genders. We engage in class warfare. Cancel culture has a thousand angles from which to attempt to bring others down, and it's always looking for more. Many of us are going on the offensive, trying to destroy others rather than taking the costly step of looking inside ourselves to figure out what the problem is and how to fix it. What we are doing to one another may not be logical, but it does serve as a very powerful diversion that keeps us from thinking about how messed up we are after casting off God's authority.

Our founders, by contrast, weren't confused about the role

God should play in society. John Winthrop, one of the first English colonists in America, called America "the city upon a hill."[12] He understood that the power source of America's greatness was its shared belief that God is real. He knew that God created us in his own image and that he bestowed on all of us certain inalienable rights. Furthermore, he understood that those who commit their wills to the will of God would come closer to finding justice and liberty than any one person or nation that did not "think it worthwhile to retain the knowledge of God" (Rom. 1:28). In other words, Winthrop and all the founders understood that we can't be good without the God who revealed himself in Scripture.

I applaud the SDS for recognizing there were injustices in America in 1962. But their failure to grasp one fact led them to embrace a philosophy that would lead us to where we are today. They failed to see the wisdom our founders had already preserved in writing, the one principle that had the potential to correct everything that was wrong with America and with any other country. You're not going to believe it, but two hundred years before *The Port Huron Statement* burst forth from the collective minds of the SDS, our founders already had a blueprint for correcting injustice:

> We hold these truths to be self-evident, that all men are created equal, that they are endowed by their Creator with certain unalienable Rights, that among these are Life, Liberty and the pursuit of Happiness.[13]

Take a moment and consider the differences between these two points of view. On the one hand, we have a group (the SDS) whose hope is in the goodness of people. But we've already made the point that, so far, people haven't demonstrated that we can be good on our own. On the other hand, our Founding Fathers believed in the goodness and fairness not of humanity but of God Almighty, our Creator.

Do you see the difference? One side believes that people are jacked up and depraved, that people cannot be trusted, that people are in desperate need of God's grace, that only a supreme and perfect God is capable of giving direction to people's steps. The other side believes that people are perfectible. They believe that people can redeem themselves by pulling themselves up by their bootstraps. Improve yourself on your own, by your own power. And if you don't join in our collective self-improvement program, if you go against the idea that we are perfectible, we will cancel you out.

Here's the problem I have with that, America. Who can live up to that standard? Who can become perfect? Who can avoid being canceled? The answer to that question is *no one*! Not when people are in charge. It is an unachievable standard that allows only one person to make it through the gauntlet of cancel culture to the top of the pyramid: the guy with the biggest stick. At least until someone else comes along with a bigger stick and beats him down and takes his place. In the case of this crowd today, the stick they use is a keyboard, lightning-fast internet service, and a large following on social media. Like the gunslingers of the Wild West who notched their pistol grips for every person they killed, these people proudly keep tally sheets of everyone they have successfully canceled.

You talk about *stress*. No wonder depression, addictions, and suicide rates are through the roof when the threat of cancellation is hanging over everyone's heads. No one is safe!

I've chosen not to participate in it or to allow it to affect me. I do mourn for those who embrace it, but I'm not intimidated by it. If you want to know why, this is it: I stand with the likes of James Madison and George Washington who did not believe that humanity was perfectible. John Adams said, "Our Constitution was made only for a moral and religious People. It is wholly inadequate to the government of any other."[14] He said this because he understood that all people are sinful and flawed, including himself, and are incapable of self-improvement. Yes, they were flawed people, but their idea that God, not government, gives us our rights was revolutionary. This idea has been the foundation for America's greatness. So I stand with them.

Before anyone says it, I am fully aware that even on the day the Declaration of Independence was put to paper, there were injustices in America. In fact, there is more than enough injustice today. I know about the unspeakable horrors of slavery and Jim Crow laws. I also know about the barbaric practice of abortion that is occurring right now, today. But if I am going to argue that these practices are unjust, where would I get the authority to make the claim that they are wrong? Would I just pull that authority out of my hat? Make it up as I go along?

Thankfully, our founders knew something that Bill Ayers and the SDS chose to ignore: God has already assigned infinite value to all of humanity. That's where I get my authority. It was God who first endowed us with inalienable rights long before the SDS appeared on the scene. Before anyone had ever heard of the SDS, the United States, or the Greek and Roman Empires for that matter, God had already gifted humanity with these rights. Neither our founders nor the SDS had anything to do with that. The only thing our founders did was to recognize these God-given rights were "self-evident." That one hyphenated word, *self-evident*, means that it should be as plain as the nose on your face that all of humanity has the right to life, liberty, and the pursuit of happiness. And since these rights are endowed by God, no one can rightfully take them away! God-endowed rights are irrevocable (that's what *inalienable* means). Even if someone else fails to honor them, we still have them because they are from God.

If you think the SDS was the first bunch to propose that people could conduct the affairs of society by allowing them to decide how we should live, you would be wrong. Two thousand years ago the apostle Paul wrote about people who bought into this philosophy eerily similar to what we see unfolding in America today:

> Furthermore, just as they did not think it worthwhile to retain the knowledge of God, so God gave them over to a depraved mind, so that they do what ought not to be done. They have become filled with every kind of wickedness, evil, greed and depravity. They are full of envy, murder, strife, deceit and malice. They are gossips, slanderers, God-haters, insolent, arrogant and boastful; they invent ways of doing evil; they disobey their parents; they have no understanding, no fidelity, no love, no mercy. (Rom. 1:28–31)

Does this sound remotely familiar? "Did not think it worthwhile to retain the knowledge of God." "Filled with every kind of wickedness, evil, greed, and depravity." "Invent ways of doing evil." Malice? Deceit? Murder? Strife? Gossip? Social media? No love? No mercy? Boastful? It sounds like I'm watching CNN. When you leave God out of the manifesto that lays out your argument for what it takes to live a good life and live free, that's a bad move. When we toss him out, God says, "Okay, I'll let you do what you want. Let's see how it works out for you." Paul said that the Almighty turns them over to a "depraved mind" when they reject him. The list in this passage is what you get. These behaviors are the natural consequences of rejecting God!

Think about it. Have you ever said, "How can people think like that?" Well, here's your answer. A depraved mind doesn't work as it was created to function. It's broken. It leads us to think the opposite of what we were created to think. For example, we were created to love God and love one another, but a depraved mind says, "I lust for wickedness! I want evil! I desire depravity and greed! I want to kill! I want to sow discord and envy! I want to pit one person against another! I loathe peace, love, and mercy! I long to fill my soul with hate! And if that isn't enough to satisfy me, I will just invent more ways of doing evil to fill my thirst for ungodliness."

We must understand that people such as this have been taken captive by Satan to do his bidding (2 Tim. 2:26). You talk about being miserable, oh, yes, it is a miserable life. The reason I know this is because I was a prisoner of this way of thinking myself (Rom. 7:23; Gal. 3:22). You talk about a hellhole, that's it. This kind of cancellation is as bad as it gets. Canceled by sin!

The problem with people who are canceled by sin and don't know it yet is that they are not content to wallow alone in the filth of their own waste. They are compelled to drag others into the pit with them. It's not enough they are headed toward destruction themselves, they must take with them as many others as possible by whatever means necessary. They are canceled, so they covet your cancellation too. The end justifies their means. Misery loves company. They will run you over. We shouldn't feel hopeless, however, because the good news is that when Christ cancels our cancellation, we are immune. We have been bathed in the blood of Christ! We are immortal! We are armed for the battle!

It's time to hit the streets, America! I am in the revolution business, but I'm not into setting other people's stuff ablaze or taking human life. You won't find me invading the United States Capitol when my candidate loses an election. No, my only goal is to destroy bad ideas that stand opposed to the knowledge of God with the gospel of truth. Trust me when I tell you, Satan won't take that lying down.

CHAPTER 3

WHO PARTICIPATES IN CANCEL CULTURE?

It is not the healthy who need a doctor, but the sick.
I have not come to call the righteous, but sinners.
Mark 2:17

Cancel culture people? Who are they?

That is a very good question. The easy answer is, almost anyone. Anyone who is frustrated with the direction of the culture can be tempted to harvest the low-hanging fruit by attacking anyone with whom they disagree. Anyone who is dissatisfied with their own moral failures can find themselves going after others to soothe their own guilty feelings. Even citizens of God's kingdom may find it easy to join the fray. If we are confused about whom we belong to, we may be tempted to jump into the game by attacking any of the symptoms of our broken culture rather than speak the truth that leads others to put their hope in Jesus. To be honest, some of the things we see going on in our culture today are indeed frightening, but we can't be confused. If we are going to walk with Christ, we must be clear about one thing: we do not belong to ourselves; we have been bought with a price (1 Cor. 6:19–20). That's why I respond to the sinful world in which I find myself by living in a way that reflects who my Master is. I don't want to misrepresent him just when the going gets tough. Remember: it's not about us but about the one who died for us.

Jesus himself encountered the cancel culture of his day, and we can learn a lot about how to react to it and who the people in cancel culture are by observing what was written about him and imitating his response. One thing I have noticed about the way he handled cancel culture is that he didn't hesitate to engage others firmly, sometimes forcefully. After reading the four Gospels

(Matthew, Mark, Luke, and John) over and over for the last forty-five years or so, I have a pretty clear idea of how Jesus handled disagreements with cancel culture.

First, I would point out that he never (not even one time) railed against the immoral. Tax collectors (a hated group of people who worked for the Romans and were considered traitors by the Jews), prostitutes, and those caught up in sexual sin were all treated with dignity. John explained why Jesus treated sinners this way in John 3:17, when he said that Jesus did not come "to condemn the world, but to save the world." Jesus knew that sinners, people on the margins of society, were well aware of their condemnation. Perhaps that is why he so quickly dispensed mercy and grace to them. They didn't need more guilt and shame; instead, they needed a way out of the filth that had become their lives. They needed hope because they were already feeling hopeless.

On the other hand, his interaction with the religious and politically connected was anything but gentle. At first glance, it would seem he went out of his way to confuse them, to make their entry into the kingdom almost impossible. Take, for example, his encounter with the Jewish leaders in John 6:48–51:

> I am the bread of life. Your ancestors ate the manna in the wilderness, yet they died. But here is the bread that comes down from heaven, which anyone may eat and not die. I am the living bread that came down from heaven. Whoever eats this bread will live forever. This bread is my flesh, which I will give for the life of the world.

If you think this sounds like he's promoting cannibalism, you are not alone. That's what the Pharisees wondered too. Of course, two thousand years later, we assume he was making a bigger point, and we would be correct. But what would be the polite and reasonable response from Jesus once he knew they had taken his words too literally. If it had been me, I would have said something like, "Hey, guys, you know I wasn't being literal, right? Let me explain." But Jesus knew his audience in ways we can never know ours. He knew what was in their minds and hearts. He had been aware of their thirst for power and control long before he ever burst from Mary's womb and was laid in a manger. So when the Jewish leaders began to grumble about his words, Jesus doubled down:

> Very truly I tell you, unless you eat the flesh of the Son of Man and drink his blood, you have no life in you. Whoever eats my flesh and drinks my blood has eternal life, and I will raise them up at the last day. For my flesh is real food and my blood is real drink. Whoever eats my flesh and drinks my blood remains in me, and I in them. Just as the living Father sent me and I live because of the Father, so the one who feeds on me will live because of me. This is the bread that came down from heaven. Your ancestors ate manna and died, but whoever feeds on this bread will live forever. (vv. 53–58)

Of course, this is the very group that wound up canceling Jesus. He knew beforehand that they had this power and would exercise it. After all, God had handed the Jewish leaders temporary power over Jesus (John 19:11). He knew they would cancel him. He also knew that without his being canceled, we would still be under the power of Satan. The Evil One would still own us. But when Christ was canceled by wicked men, our uncancellation was complete and permanent. God knew this ahead of time and gave them authority over Jesus for our sake.

Yes, Jesus knew these leaders were hard-hearted, cold, and calculating. Unwilling to submit to God's authority, they established their own regulations that would allow them to exercise control. And because they were out of harmony with the will of God, their anger at those who challenged the authority they assumed for themselves constantly simmered, ready to boil over at a moment's notice. So Jesus responded with language that left no doubt about his desire to shock them into repentance. He was well aware of their capacity for fits of rage; still, he pressed on, making sure they had an opportunity to know that only by consuming Jesus, by feeding off his every word, would they ever find fulfillment.

From the day Cain took the life of his godly brother until the present day, this is the source of cancel culture: rage. If you've ever wondered where the anger comes from, this is it. It pours out from hearts that are unwilling to submit to God and have fellowship with him. We were created to be in submissive fellowship with God, and when we aren't, we look for scapegoats to bear the guilt of our sin. It's a cheap substitute for looking inward at our own hearts and repenting of our own sins, but we have been convinced that it will do the trick. The problem with that approach is this: it never works. Attacking others may relieve the pain of our broken relationship with God for a moment, but it doesn't solve our problem for the same reason that getting drunk doesn't relieve the pain that leads one to drink. From the moment the first angry words spew from our wicked lips until the one we attack is destroyed, we are still guilty. Nothing changes! Sin can never be paid for by canceling others; only Christ's blood can do that.

But that's the world we live in. This has been our default position since the creation of the world. In the twenty-first century, however, attacking others has taken on a new viciousness as our culture shifts away from faith in the Almighty. I guess you could say that canceling others has become mainstream.

In January 2021, it occurred to me that cable television news shows had made their millions by manipulating the anger of the masses. Most of the talking heads who call themselves journalists weren't in any pursuit of truth. They didn't care about people such as you and me; they were only interested in exploiting our frustration with our culture for the sake of ratings. The angrier they could make us, the more we watched. The more we watched, the angrier we became. They knew the more we tuned into their shows, the more money they would make. So, on January 6, 2021, I told Miss Kay, "I'm done with cable news." I went back to the programming that has always entertained me: westerns! I especially enjoy movies based on the works of Louis L'Amour. He was a man who understood the world for what it was. I'd call him a wise man. One of my favorite L'Amour quotes is, "Anger is a killing thing: it kills the man who angers, for each rage leaves him less than he had been before—it takes something from him."[1]

Rage doesn't really offer a logical remedy. Rage and hostility never correct wrongs, *ever*! In fact, anger only begets more anger. Hostility may intimidate the masses into keeping their mouths shut or stirring them into a sort of mob mentality, but it never redeems a culture. The kind of unbridled anger I'm talking about steals our joy and robs us of hope. When we continue to feed it little pieces of our hearts and minds, we lose our identity, and our identity becomes our rage. Unfortunately, the more our culture slithers away from God, the more we will see this rage erupt as one unwashed sinner after another tries to shake off their shame by projecting guilt on someone else. Remember this: there are no solutions to society's ills without trusting the God who made us. Sadly, rage blinds us to that truth because it is rooted in self-reliance.

This is why Jesus dealt with the rich and powerful leaders so abruptly. They had insulated themselves with a hard shell of self-reliance. They saw no need for a suffering and serving savior. In their minds, they had everything they needed, they had it all figured out. But Jesus knew the harder the nutshell, the harder one has to strike it to get to the meat. But I don't want us to make the mistake of assuming Jesus had no interest in the salvation of the cancel culture of his day. Take a gander at his lament in Matthew 23:37:

> Jerusalem, Jerusalem, you who kill the prophets and stone those sent to you, how often I have longed to gather your children together, as a hen gathers her chicks under her wings, and you were not willing.

What do you see in Jesus' plea? Do you see his longing, his desire for the leaders of Israel? Do you hear the pain in his voice, his sorrow that the Jewish leaders had forsaken the God they claimed to serve? Ironically, he spoke these words at the conclusion of a scathing rebuke of the Jewish leaders whom he referred to as snakes, whitewashed tombs full of dead bones, blind guides, and hypocrites (among other uncomplimentary words). In the vernacular of the rednecks of North Louisiana, he raked them over the coals. He wasn't complimenting them, but he did want his harsh words to impact them in such a way that they would repent and return to him to be gathered under his wings.

If we are tormented by the tactics of cancel culture, we have only one choice if we wish to have any hope of neutralizing its impact. We must recognize that people who attack others are people with no purpose or direction. We must remember the reason they are so lacking in purpose is that they don't know the God who died for them. They have no idea that the God who made them also longs for them, desires them. Jesus understood this completely. Only hours away from breathing his last breath, he prayed for the ones who had driven the nails into his hands and feet: "Father, forgive them, for they do not know what they are doing" (Luke 23:34).

This is who the cancel culture crowd is. They are people who don't know God, and as a result, they are filled with chaos, confusion, and anger. I'm not mad at them any more than Jesus was when he prayed for their forgiveness (even though they hadn't asked for it).

And I am not angry at the journalists who characterize people such as me as narrow minded and brainwashed. After the 2020 election, so-called journalists and left-leaning pundits began to talk about reprogramming or deprogramming people such as me. Joe Hagan, a writer for *Vanity Fair* magazine, wondered, "The question is whether Trump's followers can be 'deprogrammed' the same way that, say, followers of Sun Myung Moon or L. Ron Hubbard have been."[2]

They reasoned there must be something wrong with someone who would vote for anyone other than their candidate. But I was thinking, *Reprogramming? What is that all about?* All I could think of were the times my television remote stopped working and Dan the butler had to push a few buttons and reprogram it for me. Then it hit me. That's exactly what they are talking about! Erasing our memories and downloading new ones, ones that conform to their worldview. They want to take control of our hard drives, our minds! Talk about cancellation!

Scary stuff, for sure, unless you know what I know. Here's

the problem with trying to reprogram someone such as me. It might work for some Trump voters, but I have already been deprogrammed and *reprogrammed*. What those who call for deprogramming me don't realize about me is that I put zero hope in Donald Trump. I liked a lot of his policies, but Trump didn't die for me. He wasn't raised from the dead for me. I've met him several times, and I found him to be a pretty nice guy in person. But one thing I know is that I could vote for him a thousand times and still be lost in my sins. He's just a man. Instead, all of my hope is in Jesus, and he alone is capable of reprogramming me.

I'm talking about radical transformation at the hands of Christ:

> Therefore, I urge you, brothers and sisters, in view of God's mercy, to offer your bodies as a living sacrifice, holy and pleasing to God—this is your true and proper worship. Do not conform to the pattern of this world, but be transformed by the renewing of your mind. (Rom. 12:1–2)

Did you catch that? When a person finally gets it through his thick skull (and we all have thick skulls) that the prevailing law in the kingdom of God is justice and mercy, it has one effect on humanity. Once we finally begin to get it, it creates an overwhelming desire to reject the pattern or worldview of the rest of our culture. It produces a desire to submit to God's worldview that naturally rises up in our hearts when we embrace him. When we begin to hear the rumors of God's grace, we understand we were saved from certain death only because he had mercy on us. It is then that thankfulness replaces our rage. Once we grasp the fact that we need far more from God than a little helping hand, our minds begin the transformation process. I don't need a makeover; I need to become a different person. In other words, we must first be deprogrammed from the faulty worldly assumptions about life and then *reprogram* our thinking that dupes us into believing we must earn our way to heaven by being good enough. We must be taught to think as God thinks. I'm sure this isn't what the *Vanity Fair* writer had in mind when he suggested deprograming us, but when I was transformed from self-reliance to reliance on the God who created everything, I became a new man who began to pursue my Savior instead of believing what the world said about him.

In my experience, this was the greatest relief of all, when I finally gave my life to Christ. I was happy to discover I was no longer responsible for figuring out what to do, where to go, and how to get there. I was even free from figuring out who the next president would be. Nor do I have to go after other sinners in order to cancel them since I'm a sinner too. Instead of canceling others, I am trying my hardest to introduce them to the one who can free them just as I was set free. Once God broke me out of the prison I had put myself in, there was nothing anyone else could do to me. Yes, the standards were higher, but I had clarity such as I didn't know was possible. Yes, the gospel was more demanding, in a sense, but I now had the Spirit of God to direct me. I was free of self-condemnation, free of condemnation from my fellow man, but most important, I finally knew that God loved me, that he wanted me. I was set free from God's condemnation. Wow! You talk about liberating! Oh, I was free all right.

Knowing that God loves us this much should lead us to remember that there is a difference between the way the world tries to get what it wants and the way people who follow God operate. Cancel culture's goal isn't to persuade but to intimidate and punish. It leaves no room for redemption, no room to correct mistakes. Once you're guilty, you're guilty *forever*. It doesn't matter whether your offense occurred last week or when you were a high school sophomore, you will never shake the guilt. The world won't let you. You may think the thing you did in tenth grade happened so long ago that no one remembers it now. Sadly, someone not only remembers it, but it has now been embellished with extra facts. You never really know, there may even be a video or a social media post.

Mimi Groves knows all about this. In 2016, she had used a racial slur in a three-second video clip she sent to a friend. Soon after enrolling as a student at the University of Tennessee in 2020 and then becoming a cheerleader, her video came to light, resulting in her dismissal from the cheerleading squad *and* the university. This is one issue I have with cancel culture: it is willing to time travel to a person's childhood if it will allow them to find the dirt it can use to destroy a reputation. Groves was obviously wrong when she made the video, but that's not my point. I'm talking about this insatiable desire to cancel someone that drives cancel culture practitioners to mine misdeeds from a person's childhood. The reason I find this practice so disturbing is that almost all of us were different people at nineteen years old than we were when we were fifteen. But cancel culture leaves no room for personal growth. In fact, according to Jimmy Galligan, the person who made Mimi's video public: "If I never posted that video, nothing would have ever happened. . . . And because the internet never forgets, the clip will always be available to watch. I'm going to remind myself, you started something. . . . You taught someone a lesson."[3]

Aside from the question of whether it was fair for a childhood video to determine a person's future, I would like to ask Jimmy Galligan: Are you sure there are no three-second moments from your teen years that would embarrass you if they were made public? If not, then you are one lucky man. Most of us are guilty of something we would be mortified by if it were splashed on the computer screens of America today.

This is one of the greatest problems with cancel culture: you have no recourse. In the cancel culture court, you are seen as undeniably guilty. Not innocent until proven guilty. There's no trial, no evidence for the defense, no room for growth. You are just guilty. Forever. Your only way out is to surrender and apologize, but even that may not be enough.

Alexi McCammond found out how devastating it can be to be judged by unwise social media posts excavated from her childhood. In 2021, she was chosen to be the new editor in chief of *Teen Vogue* magazine. She would have been the third African American woman to lead the magazine. I'm going to have to confess I neither knew who Alexi was nor what this magazine was all about until I did a little reading. What I discovered is that within days of securing this editorial position, she was summarily fired because an old teenage tweet surfaced in which she said she hoped she wouldn't wake up with "swollen, Asian" eyes.[4]

As I said earlier, I don't walk around planet Earth looking for ways to be offended. I'm certainly no expert on determining what is offensive, but I can tell you this: time traveling back to someone's teen years and digging up old sins to use against them today is a special kind of cruel. As I said before, I have yet to meet anyone who is not ashamed of something they did in their teen years. At an age when the part of the brain that controls impulsive behavior isn't fully developed, we are all capable of profound stupidity. I don't know about you, but I don't want anyone digging that deeply into my sinful youthful past.

God's appeal is far different from that of cancel culture. To anyone who reads the Bible with an open mind, it's apparent that we are all faulty beings. The Bible's foundation is built on one truth: humanity is inherently evil. That's why we need a savior. Jesus didn't begin his ministry by scouring the land for good people to recruit for his kingdom. In fact, the overarching theme of Jesus' ministry was, "It is not the healthy who need a doctor, but the sick" (Mark 2:17). Am I the only one who finds it ironic that if anyone ever possessed the moral superiority to hold another person's past against them, it would be God? Can you think of anyone, other than Jesus, who has the right to tell a person, "Hey, you remember that thing you did way back in [fill in your most disgusting year]? Well, that totally disqualifies you! No redemption! No forgiveness! No credit for time served or for personal growth or maturity. You are henceforth and forevermore *canceled*"? Even though God has that right, I am grateful that his love compelled him to take a different approach to my sin. Rather than permanent cancellation, he paid the penalty for my sin himself. Imagine that. The only one who had the absolute right to cancel me chose to uncancel me at his own expense.

Canceling other people is what we revert to when we are ignorant of God's love; it's just what we do. We default to it because it is a cheap substitute for faith in a merciful God. We foolishly and illogically believe we will successfully be able to play God ourselves. That is what our flesh demands; we want to be God. Even though being humble before God and admitting our guilt is the only path to freedom from guilt, we somehow figure replacing God and making up our own rules is the best path forward. This kind of whacked-up thinking began in the garden of Eden when Satan tempted Eve with one thought: you can be God (Gen. 3:4–5)! So rather than beating our chests and bowing down before God in humble submission, begging for mercy, we stiffen our backs, look around for a nearby flawed individual, and thank God we are not like that poor sinner. Then we marginalize them and cancel them (Luke 18:9–14). I suppose it makes us feel a little better for a moment or two.

But I've noticed that people who cancel others don't seem to be all that happy. If you spent just a few moments watching the newscasts of the rioters from Antifa, BLM, and the people who broke into the Capitol, you didn't see a happy throng of joyful people. Instead, you heard cursing! You saw rocks and Molotov cocktails being hurled at the police and buildings. You heard f-bombs exploding and saw that vile word spray-painted all over the place. Raging, cursing, violent crowds all yelled at the top of their voices, "You are guilty! They are guilty!" But I've never seen anyone protest against their own sin. Not once have I ever seen anyone hold a protest sign that said, "I'm a sinner!"

Trust me when I tell you there's no future for you in this. Condemning others will not add one speck of goodness to your life. You will not be happier. In fact, you'll be more miserable than you were before because you were not created to cancel but to uncancel others by loving them enough to tell them about the only one who has ever been good: Jesus! You were saved to tell others about the one who can liberate all of us from our addiction to sin and failed self-reliance.

Why is it so important to know who is behind cancel culture? To begin with, it's important to know who these people are because chances are, you and I have at some point been a part of this crowd. It's also critical to know who they are because it keeps us from being blindsided by any attacks that might come our way. Knowing who they are should lead us to another question: Where is cancel culture headed? To answer that question, I have some good news and some bad news. Which do you want first?

The bad news is that canceling others is such a powerful distraction from our own guilt that it's like an opioid. It is the fentanyl of all sins because it provides cover for our own guilt. You can check this out in Genesis; it was the second sin of Adam and Eve: they blamed someone else. Adam blamed his wife, and she blamed the serpent (Gen. 3:6–13). It's just what we do when God isn't guiding our steps: we project our guilt on someone or something else. The cancel culture is a feeble and doomed attempt to lay our personal blame at someone else's feet, anything to deflect our own guilt and project it onto others. Just keep it away from us.

So the answer is, it will probably get worse before it gets better. Their attempts at canceling you will lead to more calls for deprogramming you. You will be marginalized. You will be spoken evil of because of your faith in Jesus (Luke 6:22–23). Once they've experienced the rush of successfully canceling so many people, there's only one way to go: they're going to ramp it up. If you think you've heard the last of them, I'm afraid you're going to be surprised and disappointed. Being persecuted just goes with the territory when you follow Jesus. But that's just the bad news.

The good news, the reason I am writing this book, is that we have a redeeming message that points sinners to the one who died for them: Christ. Our story can impart to them what they've all been seeking all along: meaning, purpose, joy. It's also good news that they can't really take anything away from us, since we've already died to ourselves and received immortality. It's good news because it promises to give us the power to live happy, happy, happy, even if everything around us is imploding, even if we are being assailed on every side.

I suppose it is important to know where these people are headed because knowing prepares us for whatever they might throw at us. At least we won't be surprised when we discover the desire to control, manipulate, and destroy has no limits, that successful canceling leads to more of the same. But I am much more concerned with my relationship with the one who lifts me above the fray, to know Christ and the power of his resurrection (Phil. 3:10). There's no way we can know in advance every particular strategy the cancel culture will use in its attempts to destroy our testimony, but we don't have to. Knowing Christ and the power of his resurrection stands on its own two feet as the antidote to anything Satan throws at us. All we have to know is that the Evil One is coming for us, and being in Christ is all the protection we need.

CHAPTER 4

WHY IS CANCEL CULTURE HAPPENING?

"You are a king, then!" said Pilate.
Jesus answered, "You say that I am a king.
In fact, the reason I was born and came into
the world is to testify to the truth. Everyone
on the side of truth listens to me."
"What is truth?" retorted Pilate.
John 18:37–38

What is truth? The Roman governor Pilate who held Jesus' life in his hands has taken it on the chin for two thousand years for asking this question. That's because when he asked it, he wasn't seriously searching for an answer. It was a cynical remark that betrayed his belief that either truth did not exist or that it could not be known. But in my opinion, there is no better question anyone can ask than this because everything in life hinges on whether truth exists and whether it can be known by us.

Not too long ago I began to hear a phrase from time to time: follow your truth. The first time I heard it was a clip of Oprah Winfrey's speech at the 2019 Golden Globes Awards.[1] As soon as I heard it, I stroked my beard and turned to Dan the butler. "Follow your truth? What in the world is she talking about?"

So I began to do a little reading on this idea of truth, and what I found will shock you. As it turns out, the definition for *truth* has slowly evolved over the past fifty or sixty years. Going back in time, I found Noah Webster's 1828 definition of *truth* in his now famous dictionary. This is only the first of twelve entries for the word:

TRUTH, noun
1. Conformity to fact or reality; exact accordance with that which is, or has been, or shall be. The *truth* of history constitutes its whole value. We rely on

the *truth* of the scriptural prophecies.
My mouth shall speak truth Proverbs 8:7.
Sanctify them through thy truth; thy word
is truth John 17:17.[2]

The definition for *truth* remained consistent well into the twentieth century. But we now find this alternate definition in the online *Cambridge Dictionary*: "A fact or principle that is thought to be true by most people."[3]

This is a subtle but major shift from Webster's 1828 definition of *truth* that left no wiggle room for personal truth. In 1828, it would have been inconceivable for someone to argue that people should follow their own truth. Truth was in "exact accordance with that which is." If someone believed something that didn't line up with reality, then what they believed wasn't the truth. It was that simple.

You don't have to be a rocket scientist to figure out that when you toy with the idea of truth, that it can be shaped and molded like putty, reality takes a big hit. When most of a culture begins to accept the possibility that reality can be a personal preference, reality sooner or later becomes meaningless. That's because a reality that is moldable isn't really reality at all.

To be honest with you, this shifting meaning of truth boggles my mind because when you get down to it, the only thing that separates us from the rest of creation is our ability to find meaning through language. I guess you could try to make an argument that animals have language too. Since I'm in the business of creating and managing a habitat for wild animals and then harvesting them (a politically correct term for killing), I have learned a lot about the animal kingdom. It's true that animals can communicate to some degree. For example, depending on the species, ducks make one sound when they are feeding and another when they are in flight.

What animals lack, however, is the ability to think about their own existence using language. I highly doubt there is a mallard hen in Canada telling her children, "Now, when we begin to head south, I want you all to listen to your daddy. And if you behave yourselves, I promise I'll show you where your great-granddaddy was almost killed by a gang of crazed duck hunters." No, all that most animals can muster is, "Here's food!" "Time to breed!" "Danger!" "Better get out of here!" "You better get away from me!"

Humans, on the other hand, think about the mystery of life: "Where did I come from?" "Where am I going?" "What happens after I die?" "How can I know good and evil?" The only way we can ask or answer these significant questions is through language. Without an ability to use language, we would be no better off than a pack of wolves looking for their next meal.

So I have to ask, if words cease to have meaning, what happens to language? If words don't really mean anything, what's their purpose? This becomes especially dangerous when you monkey with the meaning of words such as *truth*. When that happens, what's the point? If I can't know what is true, how can I know what is real? If I can't know what is real, how can I know what is true? If I say "truth" but you hear "personal preference," how can we understand anything?

I would argue that we wouldn't understand. We wouldn't know anything at all. There's a segment of our culture that has lost its connection with reality. If you're wondering why some folks are talking about self-identifying as this or that, this is why. Language has become moldable. We can make it say what we want it to say.

For example, Rachel Anne Dolezal has for years claimed she is African American, and she even headed the Spokane chapter of the National Association for the Advancement of Colored People (NAACP). Her story began to unravel in 2015 when a local reporter questioned her about the African American she claimed was her father. But she refused to answer the question and even ran away from the reporter. Then Maureen Dolan and Jeff Selle reported they had discovered Dolezal had been born to very white parents who denied her claims that she was black.[4]

Dolezal was born and raised Caucasian, but she so desperately wanted to be black that she began to identify as such. Never mind her feigning blackness was an affront to millions of African Americans who had actually suffered through the discriminatory laws of the Jim Crow era; she wanted to be black. Who has a right to tell her that she can't be? Of course, none of this actually changed the truth, the reality of her ethnicity. She was born and raised white and remains so to this day. It can be proven scientifically. One DNA test proves it one way or the other.

But this is what happens when we tinker with the meaning of language—we lose connection with reality. We become confused, and with the confusion, we lose joy and peace and meaning because of an inner voice that tells us that nothing is real. The only way life can mean anything at all is for us to know that we've embraced reality. When we lose reality, we lose everything.

The Beatles described this dilemma perfectly in their song "Strawberry Fields Forever." They dreamed of a world in which reality is an illusion. It is an alternate universe where we can't really know anything at all.

What a hopeless and meaningless worldview. Nothing is real. Living is easy with our eyes closed. No wonder my generation slithered off into a land where confusion and chaos rule the day. Nothing is real? What a crock. No one really believes this. You can tell me all day long that you don't believe in objective truth (truth that is unchangeable and not subject to opinion), but you don't behave as if you really believe it. No one does.

I've observed the crowd who promote this distorted view of reality are the angriest and most self-righteous people I have ever seen. But why? If truth and reality are moldable according to our personal preferences, if nothing is real, why cancel culture? For example, why would you cancel Drew Brees for stating his love for the flag? If truth is personal, isn't his truth just as valid as your truth? If Brees's reality is that Americans should respect "The Star-Spangled Banner," who's to say he should be canceled for his opinion? If truth is relative, and J. K. Rowling's truth is that womanhood is defined by biology and DNA, why attack her for expressing her truth? If we are honest with ourselves, we would have to admit the concept of moldable truth is illogical and unsustainable. The idea that truth and reality can mean what we want them to mean falls in on itself. It cannot bear its own weight. The idea that truth is fluid may sound good in theory, but I've never met anyone who lives as if that were actually true. No wonder so many folks are enraged in modern America. They can't make sense of their own worldview.

You may be rightly thinking this is all nonsense. You also may be asking where in the world it all came from. How in the world could a concept such as truth, which has always meant that which conforms to reality, come to mean anything else? The short answer is that when we reject God, we reject reality. But why would anyone want to reject reality? Why would anyone want to reject God? The apostle Paul answered that question:

The wrath of God is being revealed from heaven against all the godlessness and wickedness of people, who suppress the truth by their wickedness, since what may be known about God is plain to them, because God has made it plain to them. For since the creation of the world God's invisible qualities—his eternal power and divine nature—have been clearly seen, being understood from what has been made, so that people are without excuse. (Rom. 1:18–20)

When we reject truth, we do so because we are looking to be emancipated from the authority of God. All of mankind's sin is rooted in the desire to be God, as Genesis 3:5 illustrates: "For God knows that when you eat from it your eyes will be opened, and you *will be like God, knowing good and evil*" (emphasis added). We want to be in charge. We want to determine how we will live. The problem with that is, to pull that off, we must first eliminate God. Of course, we can't actually do that, so we have to convince ourselves that we have. But according to Paul, the difficulty in eliminating God is that we must first eliminate the mystery and majesty of creation. When I walk in the woods that I manage as a wildlife habitat, I marvel at the majesty and creative power of God. But someone who wants to be liberated from God's authority must develop an ability to look at the same thing and say, "There is no God. This all just happened by chance." In order to do our own thing, we must first eliminate the ultimate source of authority: almighty God. Or if we don't completely eliminate him, we must neuter him, make him impotent. In other words, our wickedness leads us to erase God or radically alter his nature and character.

The problem with truth and reality being fluid is that no one's ever really certain about what is real. How can we know anything? As I said earlier, we can say we believe truth and reality are personal, but we never behave as if we really believe that. This is especially true of the cancel culture crowd. With them, the goalpost keeps moving because their reality is constantly shifting. I've noticed most of them make no appeal to the authority of God when they condemn, yet they sound so moralistic and self-righteous. Their attacks seem to appeal to some unchangeable standard of truth, yet that standard is elusive, ever changing. We can't even keep up with the rules.

The issue I have with people who are constantly on the attack, who seem hell-bent on destroying others, is that they usually lack connection with the one being who can restore a sense of order to their understanding of reality: God Almighty. At one time I had lost connection with the God of the universe too. That's why I'm not angry with them. I understand them. It's my hope that more of them will come to their senses, as I did. But it's important they understand they have embraced an illogical and unsustainable view of truth. Just as I did forty-five years ago, they must reach the inescapable conclusion that their personal reality is leading them nowhere. When truth is not rooted in what is real, we grasp at straws trying to make sense of the universe. What we find is that we are angrier, more jealous, more self-righteous, and less joyful.

So what's the solution?

As it turns out, Scripture has a lot to say about truth, but there is one passage that, when we begin to grasp how significant it is, has the power to radically and unalterably change the direction of our lives. Just days before Jesus was led off to be executed, he was giving his disciples some last-minute instructions. He told them: Don't let your hearts be troubled! Trust God! Trust me! I'm going to prepare a place for you! I'll be back for you! Then he said something that confused some of them. "You know the way to the place where I am going" (John 14:4).

Of course, this ragtag band of followers was clueless about what he meant. They were looking at one another and back at Jesus and mumbling, "What's he talking about? We don't know where he's going. We didn't even know that he was going. So how are we going to know the way?"

Then Jesus handed them the road map. No, they didn't understand it was a road map at first. They only grasped that fact after they had seen his resurrected body and received the Holy Spirit. But it was a road map for sure, one that would guide them the rest of their lives. After the day of Pentecost (Acts 2), this bunch would never be confused again. They would remember what he said:

I am the way and the truth and the life. No man comes to the Father except through me. (John 14:6)

When Jesus said this, he wasn't defining the truth about the way, as if it were an abstract concept. He wasn't saying, "I will tell you the truth!" He was actually saying, "*I am* the truth." Look up *truth* in heaven's dictionary, and it has a one-word definition: Jesus. Hang in here with me because this may all sound a little deep at first, but it isn't really.

You may be wondering why this is important. It matters because it is impossible for us to have a relationship with a concept. When truth is just a concept, it is a cold and sterile thing. It doesn't really change our hearts. A transformed heart before God happens only when we come to Jesus as the embodiment of truth. He doesn't just tell the truth, he *is* truth.

When I came to Jesus as a person (instead of as an idea), I had to come to the end of my own self and admit I had been chasing all the wrong things. I confessed I had made a complete mess of my life by following my own truth, that I had embraced delusions rather than reality. I had to admit I had created a universe I thought I wanted, but it turned out to be a horrible nightmare. When I got to this point, when reality became real again, when real truth became a priority to me, I turned around. I repented.

When I saw Jesus as the way, the truth, and the life, I embraced him. I also simultaneously embraced a love for reality, a love that says, "I'll follow you anywhere because you are the truth and the life. I'll follow you because you are real. I'll believe you!" Instead of telling ourselves to stop sinning, we trust that Christ isn't holding out on us. We realize that everything he has ever told us is something we can bank on because he is truth!

Something else Jesus said about his followers just before his death is important to note:

I am coming to you now, but I say these things while I am still in the world, so that they may have the full measure of my joy within them. I have given them your word and the world has hated them, for they are not of the world any more than I am of the world. My prayer is not that you take them out of the world but that you protect them from the evil one. They are not of the world, even as I am not of it. Sanctify them by the truth; your word is truth. (John 17:13–17)

Since Jesus is the embodiment of truth, his words can be trusted as true. If I am unaware that God is reliable and that I can trust his Word as truth and the only path to reality, I'm going to be tossed about in the waves of culture. This is exactly what Paul was talking about in Ephesians 4:14: "Then we will no longer be . . . tossed back and forth by the waves, and blown here and there by every wind of teaching and by the cunning and craftiness of people in their deceitful scheming."

In other words, if you and I want to avoid the lies and false realities of Satan, who does not have our best interests at heart, then we must be full of Christ, full of truth (Eph. 4:13). When Christ lives in us, we seek his voice because we are certain his Word is the Word of Life. When Christ tells me to love my enemies, for example, I pray for the strength to do it.

Before I admitted I had purposely chased after lies, I was a horrible husband, a horrible father, a horrible son, a horrible brother, and a horrible friend. If you ask me now if I loved my family back then, I wouldn't really know how to answer. Sure, I guess I had some affection for them, but the lies I believed kept me in the dark about what real love was. When I came to the realization that my life was spiraling out of control and that perhaps I should believe Jesus, everything changed. So when I saw that God told me to love my wife as Christ loves the church, I desired to do that, not because it was easy, but because I learned to trust the Word of God, the voice of God. I trusted I was being told the truth because Christ said it. And I trusted that he never lies and he would never lead me to any place that would do me harm. Believe me when I tell you that my relationship with Miss Kay took on a new passion once I prayed for God to empower me to love her in this way. If you don't believe me, ask her. She sure doesn't mind telling folks about my former way of life.

The alternative to trusting Jesus' Word is that we will be forced to attempt to navigate the murky waters of life on our own, trying to find some glimmer of truth we can latch on to. But at the end of the day, this isn't much. Just a morsel of truth here and there isn't going to get the job done. I'm going to need much more than that if I'm going to live with purpose and confidence.

I need to be in fellowship with the one who never changes and who always does the right thing. I need the truth! In other words, I need Jesus.

Living without an objective standard of truth—truth that doesn't change—has horrible consequences. The first casualty of a truthless worldview is the value of humanity itself. God said we matter because we bear his image. The unguided worldview, the godless worldview, has no real basis for saying that individuals matter. It may pay lip service to the idea that people matter, but how could it make that argument if we are not created beings who carry God's DNA in every cell? If you have ever wondered how an enlightened people could murder sixty-two million unborn children over the last forty-eight years, this is it.[5] In a godless world of moldable truth, someone's going to get hurt, because we don't have a way to figure out what a person's value is.

The difference is that when I point out that someone's behavior is not based on truth, I'm not appealing to the latest buzz words used by cancel culture: respect, inclusion, decency, integrity, harmony, peace. These are good words, and they are attributes I strive for, but not just because they are words. They've been hijacked and used as weapons to cancel. I strive to display them in my life because they reflect the nature of Christ. When I began to see Jesus as the truth and agreed to follow him, I automatically became more like him. I became more inclusive, decent, honest, harmonious, and peace loving.

Unlike the standard much of the world submits to, the one I try to live by is not subject to change. And if I'm right, that Jesus is the truth and that his Word is true, I'm not just pulling moral standards out of thin air. God has revealed truth to me by his Word. I am committed to preaching Jesus and his Word because I know that the end result of living a life committed to anything or anyone else is doomed. The prophet Isaiah said as much:

> What sorrow for those who say
>> that evil is good and good is evil,
> that dark is light and light is dark,
>> that bitter is sweet and sweet is bitter. (5:20 NLT)

A life based on the idea that reality is moldable is a miserable one. So it's my aim to destroy falsehoods that lead people away from the truth, away from Jesus Christ who was killed for our sins and raised from the dead. I'm not about cancellation except that I want to see meaningless and directionless lives canceled. Miss Kay and I have been blessed to have witnessed thousands of people turn away from the lie that truth is personal to embrace the one who speaks the Word of Truth. Addicts who rejected drugs in favor of Christ-centered sobriety, prostitutes whose eyes were opened to the purpose God had for them as daughters of the Almighty, and unfaithful spouses who finally saw that sexual fulfillment could only be realized in a godly marriage. We've rejoiced as lives have gone from hopeless to hopeful simply because they committed themselves to the Spirit of truth.

When we love the one who said that he is "the way and the truth and the life," we begin to live as free men and women. I say free because this kind of love for Christ liberates us from the bondage of sin. It frees us from our addiction to the lies of Satan. It puts us into a relationship with truth because it is centered on the personhood of Jesus. This, my friends, is a message that will change the world. At least it will radically alter the direction of anyone's life who rejects falsehood and embraces Christ.

Will there be people who won't take the truth lying down?

You can bet everything you have on that. Oh, they'll come after you all right. When cynical and unbelieving people echo Pontius Pilate (What is truth?), what do we expect will happen when we respond with the name of Jesus? The good news for me is that when a few of them turn away from untruth and turn to Christ, I know I am doing the work of God. I'll just continue to love and pray for those who oppose me since they aren't really opposing me but rather the one who is the way and the truth and the life. I've already determined that going with Jesus is worth whatever it costs me:

> What good will it be for someone to gain the whole world, yet forfeit their soul? (Matt. 16:26)

Like a marriage in which the partners have drifted apart, I want to turn to America and ask her, "What happened to us? We were doing so well, and now we are on the brink of breaking up." As Paul told the Galatians, "You were running a good race. Who cut in on you to keep you from obeying the truth?" (Gal. 5:7).

The reason this matters is because the root of cancel culture is a disdain for truth. It is rooted in a hatred for the authority and sovereignty of God. It is born out of that desire we talked about to be our own gods. But here comes Jesus, claiming that he is the truth in person, claiming that we can find truth nowhere else except in him. And his message to mankind is that if they want in on real truth, they must surrender everything they have and everything they are in order to follow him. Coming to Jesus as the provider of truth is an admission we have failed miserably and are under a death sentence that only the blood of Christ can remove. This is where the rubber meets the road, the point of decision where we decide whether or not Jesus is worth following. It will be the hardest decision you will ever make because it violates your desire to be your own god. But in my experience, it is the best decision you can ever make.

Yes, the gospel is offensive to those who do not love reality. To people who do not want to admit their own moral failure and fall down before Christ, the gospel is not complimentary. When it comes to people opposing us when we proclaim the truth of the gospel, what did we expect would happen? Hey, if they canceled Jesus, they'll cancel his followers too. Even so, it's not our job to cancel the people in cancel culture. Our responsibility is to make certain that our commitment to the pursuit of reality and truth is firm and to convince others to do the same. If it is, we will live contentedly and joyfully in an angry, chaotic world.

CHAPTER 5

WHO'S THE BOSS?

She will give birth to a son, and you are
to give him the name Jesus, because he
will save his people from their sins.

Matthew 1:21

At some point in the early 1980s, I found myself standing before a large crowd at a sporting goods expo at the Louisiana Superdome. Over my head and behind me was a large banner that read Budweiser: The King of Beers. To be honest, most of the crowd gathered around me had imbibed a little more Budweiser than they should have, if you get my drift. I went through my usual routine of blowing the duck calls dangling from my lanyard, explaining which species each of the calls was designed to attract. I concluded with a few hunting stories and placed the lanyard with the duck calls in my mud-stained knapsack.

Apparently, some of the rednecks in the audience figured I was finished with my presentation and turned away. But what I did next stopped them in their tracks. I retrieved my Bible from my bag, cocked my head to one side, and held it up while sporting my best "What's this?" look. The well-worn book was held together with duct tape. Loose sheets of yellow legal paper with notes from my Bible studies fell to the stage as I opened it. After a few seconds, I spoke as boldly and as loudly as I could: "Boys, look what I have here. It looks like I brought my Bible with me. No sense in letting it go to waste." At that point I laid down a gospel presentation like you've never heard.

You're probably wondering what the response from the crowd was. To be honest, some of them scurried away in disgust. I imagined that some of them said as they walked hurriedly from the room, "I get enough of this religious crap from my wife and her preacher. I don't need to hear it here." But others stayed and listened with attentive ears. The story I told that day cut some of them to the bone.

I explained how every human being who ever set foot on this planet was sinful, and because of their sin, they were condemned. I hammered on some of the sins listed in Galatians 5 just to make sure they got the message: sleeping around with women you aren't married to, wild partying and drunkenness and drug use, jealousy, fits of rage, sowing discord and gossip, and envy. I quoted a short passage: "Those who live like this will not inherit the kingdom of God" (v. 21). Then I told them, "Some of you spend your whole life trying to get drunk, get high, and get laid. How's that working out for you?" I tried to hit each of those sins in a way that left no doubt that most of the men in that crowd stood guilty before God.

It did not escape my attention that a few of them began to nervously shift from one foot to the other as if searching for a way to escape the firestorm the message was raining down on them. I'm thankful that most of them hung around for the good news.

Since I didn't have any notes, I don't recall my exact words, but my story has been basically the same for more than forty years. "Boys, even though you stand condemned before God and deserve hell, do I ever have some good news for you." From there I told them about the Son of God who came to earth, took on human form, was brutalized by his creation, and hung on a cross until he was dead. I told them about the resurrection of Christ's physical body from the tomb only three days later. I implored them to accept God's offer of free mercy and grace. I told them they should repent of their sins, give control of their lives to Jesus, and find someone to dunk them in some water in order to identify with the death, burial, and resurrection of Jesus. I said, "Die to your sins, symbolically bury the old man, and rise up to walk a new life" (Rom. 6:1–4).

At the moment I didn't exactly know the impact my little presentation would have on the crowd. Knowing human nature as I do, I figured some of them might hear it and turn to God, but I figured most of them would walk away unscathed. When I arrived back home in West Monroe, however, the phone began to ring.

"I don't know what you did to my husband, but he walked through the door, fell to his knees, and began to weep and plead for my forgiveness." I received several calls over the next few days that said essentially the same thing. So I began to ponder the significance of this. I wondered what impact I could have on the kingdom of God if I boldly proclaimed the good news of Jesus every time I was invited to speak somewhere. It didn't take me long to make the decision to do just that. I would never speak again without preaching Jesus before I left.

When I shared my plan with some of my advisors, a few of them said, "Hey, you can't mix business and religion. If you do, you'll lose them both." I smiled and said, "We shall see, boys! We shall see!" What they didn't know is that before I left the Superdome, five preachers had come to me and whispered, "That was an incredible message. Would you come to my church and preach?" That began a run of nationwide public speaking engagements that lasted for more than fifteen years. I wasn't famous. In fact, not many people knew anything about me outside of duck hunting circles. It was as simple as this: my boldness led to many opportunities to tell people about Jesus.

Once in a while I would get an invitation to speak at some event where the person calling me would qualify my invitation with, "We'll pay you well, but we don't want you to preach." My response was always the same, "Sorry, but that's what I do." I'm happy to report I never missed a meal. I just continued to preach Jesus everywhere I went, without considering the personal consequences.

You may be wondering what's so important about Jesus that a guy like me would unashamedly tell the story of the gospel wherever he goes. The truth is that when I was wallowing in the filth of my own sin and depravity, I had no idea how much Jesus had sacrificed on behalf of my worthless hide. I'm not just talking about his death on the cross but how far he had to travel in order to become like me. Just think about it. A God who would leave the throne room of heaven and become a human being? A God who would die for his rebellious creation? I just couldn't figure out why he would subject himself to the ridicule and violence of human beings over whom he had complete authority and power.

At the time, it was hard for me to imagine because I was nothing like that. At my immediate disposal were any number of firearms I would have discharged at a moment's notice if anyone tried to do me harm. But I kept hearing about the Creator of the universe willingly allowing weak and miserable people to mistreat him and nail him to a cross. I kept wanting him to fire off a few lightning bolts and call on a vast army of powerful angels and destroy the holier-than-thou Jewish leaders who had manipulated the crowds into crying out, "Crucify him! Crucify him!" I wanted a Chuck Norris kind of God, I suppose.

So when you ask why I'm so bold, this is it. I am bold because I am convinced that God's love for me is so potent it compelled Jesus to leave the glories of heaven. He descended to this sin-cursed planet to redeem me, to buy me back from the Evil One who had taken me captive to do his will instead of God's.

Think about it. If I had discovered the cure for Alzheimer's or cancer, would I be timid in telling others about it? No, I wouldn't care who was offended by it, I would break my neck to make sure everyone who needed the cure at least had an opportunity to receive it. But even then, I would only be postponing the inevitable. Everyone dies. When it comes to the gospel, however, I have been given the Word of Life, eternal life.

In other words, I am bold in preaching Jesus because I am so grateful for what he's done for me. And the more I understand the enormous value of the gift he's given me by cleansing me from my moral filth, the more I want to tell the story. It's a privilege for me to publicly tell of the majesty and love of God. I am unashamed because the gospel demonstrates the power of God like nothing else can. "For I am not ashamed of the gospel, because it is the power of God that brings salvation to everyone who believes: first to the Jew, then to the Gentile" (Rom. 1:16).

It's powerful, not in a Chuck Norris kind of way, but because it has the power to do what no one else and nothing else could do for mankind. It is powerful because it gives hope to the hopeless. The gospel is hopeful like nothing else. It's a hope that promises to reunite me with my parents and five siblings who have already gone to the grave. Hope that I will be free from the spiritual and physical shackles that have weighed me down. The gospel is a hope that my past won't define my future. It gives me hope that my sin is not greater than God's mercy.

With a message like this, why would I be timid in telling it? Everyone needs hope. I've encountered them all: drug addicts, divorced people, folks with anger issues, murderers, gossips, slanderers, thieves, and people caught up in sexual addictions and perversions. Lives destroyed by sin. The gospel is for the people who've given up and resigned themselves to the thought that this is just how it is. I've had a great life, but the thought occurred to me, *Is this all there is?* If I didn't know Jesus, the answer would be yes. This is all there is, and it's meaningless.

By contrast, the world offers no hope. If we were to take a random survey of some people on the street and ask them what it would take to make them happy, how do you think most people would respond? We both know that most people would say money, fame, possessions, and health would bring them joy. But have you ever wondered why so many wealthy, famous, healthy, and beautiful people are the most miserable? It's because being a consumer of the things of this world will never fill the void that is in every human heart. It's impossible for things to make us happy because we know deep down, inside our gut, all of those things are destined to perish. None of it will last until the water gets hot.

We know about people who had everything we think we need to make us happy, yet they died with a cloud of hopelessness over their heads. Robin Williams, Whitney Houston, Michael Jackson, Elvis Presley, Janis Joplin, Jimi Hendrix. The list could go on and on. But all of them had two things in common: every one of them had it all and they all died feeling hopeless. As it turns out, they were no different from the rest of us. Consuming the things of this world never brought them the fulfilment Satan promised.

It's not just the jacked-up people who can find hope in Jesus, though. When I preach his name, I also want the church members who are just going through the motions to know about Jesus. Somewhere out there are respectable businesspeople who have just discovered that money and success have failed to make them happy. I want them to know Jesus. At some point, all of us have been disappointed by the promises of the world. I don't care who you are or what you've done. I don't even care if you've attacked me and tried to cancel me (and neither does Jesus). I still want you to know him. I want you to know him because I know that without him you have no hope. You are living a miserable life of hopelessness, even if you are doing it in secret.

Since I'm telling people about the one person who can give purpose to their temporary lives, I'm not fearful of anything mankind could throw at me for preaching Jesus. The way I figure it, I'm doing folks a favor by pointing them to Christ, who came to serve mankind.

In your relationships with one another, have the same mindset
as Christ Jesus:

Who, being in very nature God,
did not consider equality with God
something to be used to his own advantage;
rather, he made himself nothing
by taking the very nature of a servant,
being made in human likeness.
And being found in appearance as a man,
he humbled himself
by becoming obedient to death—
even death on a cross! (Phil. 2:5–8)

You talk about boldness? This is as bold as it gets. Even though Jesus didn't exercise physical power to win his battles, he was not powerless. All he had to do was say the word, and the Father would have sent an army of angels to save him. *Whoosh!* The angels would have swept in, and that would have been the end of the Roman Empire, the Jewish leadership, and all of mankind. But they weren't his focus because they (the Romans and the Jews) were just lackeys for the one who was really in charge.

His power was reserved for the ruler of hell who had kept us all captive to our pasts. He was clear about his purpose. Instead of bringing condemnation, he came to serve you and me. I'm not saying he came to be our personal assistant, like we could just order him to bring us a glass of tea. He didn't come to help us find an open spot in a crowded parking lot. Instead, he came to serve us by dying in our place. He came to serve by paying the penalty for our sin. He is our servant because he gave up everything to accomplish for us what we could not do for ourselves.

Yes, he gave it all up for us! The only prerequisite for entering his kingdom is this:

> In the same way, those of you who do not give up everything you have cannot be my disciples. (Luke 14:33)

From where I sit, giving up everything I have to follow Jesus is a no-brainer. That's because all of the junk I can give up has already proved it can never satisfy me. All of it—health, youth, money, possessions, fame—has already begun to perish. They've lost their luster or disappeared altogether. Put my hope in Jesus or put it in all the things of this world? What should I do? I'll take Jesus for ten thousand, Alex. I'll follow the bold one who knows the true value of putting my trust in him.

Bold? No, I'm not really bold. I just preach a bold Savior. I am unafraid because he is unafraid to point out the failings of human constructs. He boldly condemned the power grab of the Jewish leaders who made it difficult for average people to know God. Bold? Could he be any more bold than to point to the crowd who had the power to kill him and call them hypocrites and blind guides? Was he bold when he called them blind fools and whitewashed tombs? Oh, that's as bold as it gets. That's who I follow!

I am bold because Jesus is bold, and he is bold because he knows the temptation that all people experience to put their hopes in things that don't matter and don't last. He violently rips falsehoods and delusions from our grasp because he is aware that these things will destroy us. He spoke boldly even though he knew the final outcome would be that powerful people would cancel him by murdering him.

The story of the gospel of Jesus is a story that changes lives because it liberates us from the bondage of self-reliance. It transports us into the kingdom of God where everything important and meaningful dwells. But what happens when people who claim to be Christ followers water him down and deny the truth of his Word? I suggest they have no message to provide hope to the hopeless. They become fearful and confused. They have nothing to offer those who are caught up in Satan's schemes.

This is what happened in early 2021 when a church in Nashville declared in a Facebook post that the Bible isn't the Word of God. They said the Bible "isn't the Word of God, self-interpreting, a science book, an answer/rule book, inerrant or infallible." Rather than being the Word of God, they said it is "a product of community, a library of texts, multi-vocal, a human response to God, living and dynamic."[1]

I understand what the first part of their statement means, that the Bible isn't the Word of God. But I'm going to be honest with you that I have no clue what "a product of community" means. "A library of texts"? "Multi-vocal"? "A human response to God, living and dynamic"? Okay, I'm thoroughly confused. Well, I would be if I didn't know one thing: when people begin to drift away from the idea that truth is discoverable and knowable in Jesus in a failed effort to be relevant to the world around them, they drift into the nonsense we find in this statement.

To be honest with you, the thought of living in a world without knowing who is in charge of things sends chills down my spine. That's because I have zero confidence in myself and my fellow human beings that we can construct a system that allows us to live harmoniously and meaningfully. Not only that, but if I accept this church's view of the Bible, what do I tell the thousands of people who have come through my door in search of the answers to life? In that case, what do I tell the drug addicts and the people on the brink of divorce? Would I be able to give any meaningful answer to anyone who asks me how they can overcome the sin that is wreaking havoc in their life? Without the Jesus of the Bible, would I be forced to direct them to the local bookstore's self-help section? I don't think so. If self-help worked, we would all be healthy by now. I know I wouldn't point them to a book this church calls a "human response to God." I don't want human responses to guide my steps; I want to hear it from the King of kings, from almighty God who spoke the universe into existence. I can trust someone like that.

Why Jesus? Why the boldness? I'm going with Jesus 100 percent of the way because only he can meet the deepest needs of mankind. He died for the sins of the world, but he also died for me. He poured out his love on me, the most undeserving of all mankind. I guess you could say I take his death personally. And by following him, I learn to be like him: passionate and bold about others knowing him. Since I follow him, I will not be deterred by the opposition. I walk with the one who was raised from the dead.

When I observe the direction of today's culture, there's a

good chance you and I will be canceled for preaching Jesus as the only hope mankind has to find purpose and meaning. When that happens, I return to the wisdom of the Word of God to give me the strength to stay strong. I've never been left hanging, not even once:

> Be on your guard; stand firm in the faith; be courageous; be strong. Do everything in love. (1 Cor. 16:13–14)

CHAPTER 6

THERE'S A VACCINE
FOR THAT!

Jesus Cancels Our Cancellation

He forgave us all our sins, having *canceled*
the charge of our legal indebtedness, which
stood against us and condemned us; he has
taken it away, nailing it to the cross.

Colossians 2:13–14, emphasis added

The German pastor Dietrich Bonhoeffer began his ministry at about the same time that Adolf Hitler rose to power. Bonhoeffer spoke out boldly against the Nazi regime. In April 1943, the Gestapo arrested Bonhoeffer and hurled him into a concentration camp to await trial. Two years later, in April 1945, just days before the camp was liberated by the Allies, he was quickly tried and convicted for his alleged role in the 1944 plot to assassinate Hitler. He was hastily executed by hanging before he could be freed.

I've already made the point that people have always had a tendency to eliminate their enemies. Just ask one of the first humans to ever inhabit planet Earth, Abel, who was slain by his brother in a fit of jealousy (Gen. 4:2–8). Ask the first Christian martyr, Stephen, who was stoned to death by the Jewish leaders (Acts 7:54–60). Cancel culture has always been there; it happens anytime anyone gets in the way of the agenda of those who lust for power and authority.

You don't have to be a saint to be a victim of cancel culture. These people are so addicted to the power that comes with it that they will attack anyone. Ask Ellen DeGeneres. One minute she was called the queen of nice and the next moment she was being attacked by brave anonymous cancelers.[1]

What was her crime? In 2019, she was spotted at a Dallas Cowboys game having a grand time in a skybox with George W. Bush. The attack from social media was vicious. One person said, "Being nice to Bush means in turn disrespecting those whose lives were destroyed by his disastrous administration. You literally cannot be kind to everyone. You have to choose a side! Ellen certainly has."[2] What a unique idea! Being nice to someone with whom you disagree.

Even though cancelers will attack anyone, it seems to me that it is Christians who suffer the most. Maybe it's because our worldview poses the greatest threat to the exercise of power and control. Remember, it's hard to control people who've already given it all up for the kingdom of God. Just take a quick look at history and you'll see thousands, maybe even millions, who have been persecuted, imprisoned, or killed for their faith. Hebrews 11 lists several faithful God lovers who were victorious over the cancel culture of their day because of their faith in a holy and righteous God. Moses refused to be identified as one of Pharaoh's sons, instead choosing to obey God and lead the Hebrews out of Egypt. In fact, he chose mistreatment over the pleasures of sin.

But the following passage also gives us examples of others who suffered simply because they refused to abandon the God who is there and bow down to whatever god was in fashion at the time:

There were others who were tortured, refusing to be released so that they might gain an even better resurrection. Some faced jeers and flogging, and even chains and imprisonment. They were put to death by stoning; they were sawed in two; they were killed by the sword. They went about in sheepskins and goatskins, destitute, persecuted and mistreated—the world was not worthy of them. They wandered in deserts and mountains, living in caves and in holes in the ground. (vv. 35–38)

After reading these accounts, perhaps you are wondering why anyone would willingly put themselves in harm's way like this. I mean, why not keep their faith in Christ private? Wouldn't it be safer to just shut your mouth about Jesus? The answer is that all of them were willing to suffer for Christ because they had faith in the work of Christ. Since they had either seen his resurrected body or knew someone who had, they had confidence in his promise to raise from the dead anyone who believed in him.

Let me back up and give you the short version of what my problem was before Christ saved me from myself. I had a virus, a deadly one. It was not comforting to me to know this virus had ushered in a worldwide pandemic, that every person on the planet was infected, because I was the one who was suffering. I was the one who was destroying his life and the lives of the people he loved most. Unfortunately, the virus eating away at my soul was incurable.

"What virus are you talking about, Phil?"

I'm talking about this virus:

> There is no one righteous, not even one;
>> there is no one who understands;
>> there is no one who seeks God.
> All have turned away,
>> they have together become worthless;
> there is no one who does good,
>> not even one.
> Their throats are open graves;
>> their tongues practice deceit.
> The poison of vipers is on their lips.
>> Their mouths are full of cursing and bitterness.
> Their feet are swift to shed blood;

ruin and misery mark their ways,

and the way of peace they do not know.

There is no fear of God before their eyes. (Rom.

3:10–18)

The virus that was ravaging me was the virus of sin. If you want a definition for sin, the best one I can give you is that I became a sinner when I announced to God he was unfit to be God and I could do a better job if I sat on his throne. It's when I called him a liar. It's when I accused him of holding out on me. Sin is rebellion, an act of treason against the kingdom of God. It's when we doubt the goodness and faithfulness of the Almighty and begin to do things our own way.

If you want to know what that looks like, just reread the passage above. Before I believed Christ, did I have understanding? That's a joke! Had I turned away? Yep! Did I do good? Not at all. Did my tongue practice deceit? Did cursing and bitterness pour forth from my lips? Was I a peaceful man? Did I fear God? Guilty! Guilty! Guilty! Truthfully, I knew I was boiling in hot peanut oil. I knew I was bound for eternal destruction. I just had no idea how I could get out of it. I thought my condemnation was a done deal.

So what did I do in response? I ran! I hid! I grabbed the first thing I could find to conceal my nakedness before God. Anything would do as long as it kept me from thinking about my virus. In my case, it was sex, drugs, and alcohol. Those were my distractions.

But one question haunted me the whole time I was running from God. *Is there hope?* I assumed I was over the limit when it came to sin. I figured God could never love a man like me. But just when I was on the verge of giving up, someone came to me with the most incredible tale. When they first told me, it sounded too good to be true, sort of like a grinning used-car salesman making his pitch.

"Do I ever have a deal for you!"

But the offer was right before me in black and white. And oddly the possibility that it could be true hit a nerve with me. What I found out about God was the exact opposite of what I thought I knew about him. He actually loves me in spite of the fact I had called him a liar:

> For the wages of sin is death, but the gift of God is eternal life
> in Christ Jesus our Lord. (Rom. 6:23)

At the time, I thought, *What? I know my life is a wreck and I deserve death, but what's this stuff about a free gift of salvation? God's just going to give it to me? Free of charge?* I was skeptical because no one had ever given me anything for free. There were always strings dangling from any gift I'd ever received. *Now you're telling me God is just going to hand it over? Eternal life? After all I've done? No way!*

God wasn't done with me, though. My sister, in an effort to save my soul, dragged a pastor into the bar I operated. And while I ridiculed them at first, this story of free gifts that Pastor Bill laid on me rocked my world. Then he hit me with the big one:

> When you were dead in your sins and in the uncircumcision
> of your flesh, God made you alive with Christ. He forgave us
> all our sins, having canceled the charge of our legal indebted-
> ness, which stood against us and condemned us; he has taken it
> away, nailing it to the cross. And having disarmed the powers
> and authorities, he made a public spectacle of them, triumphing
> over them by the cross. (Col. 2:13–15)

I thought, *I don't know who wrote this, but he must have known me.* Was I dead? Without a doubt! Was I sinful? Had I violated the written code? Had I broken the regulations? Was the law I had broken a constant reminder I was a sinner? Yes to all of that!

In my heart, I already knew this. What I didn't know was what Pastor Bill told me next. I don't remember his exact words, but I remember the gist of it. I'm still clear about that.

"Phil, you're going to love what I'm going to tell you next," he said. "You know that little voice in your head that is telling you that you are too far gone for God? That you've crossed the line? Well, it's true that you have crossed the line and that you are too far gone to enter the throne room of God. It's also true you can do nothing about it. The death sentence you have hanging over your sorry head must be paid. You've been *condemned*! But the Almighty has taken care of your problem. He took your debt, along with the legal code that condemns you because you violated it, and he nailed them both to the cross."

What? A filthy sinner like me? The Son of God died in my place? He has restored immortality to me? To me? A sexually promiscuous alcoholic drug user like me? While Pastor Bill didn't say it exactly this way, what he was telling me was that God had canceled my cancellation. God had vaccinated me against the virus that was killing me, and that vaccination came from the veins of the body of Jesus.

Now back to the question of why anyone would publicly speak the name of Jesus when the cancel culture crowd is hovering over humanity like vultures, looking for anyone to devour. In my opinion, it's a no-brainer. When confronted with the options of keeping my mouth shut in a vain attempt to avoid cancellation or telling people about the one who paid the debt I had hanging over my head, I'm going with Jesus every single time.

That's because when I came to Christ, I willingly gave it all up to follow him. I didn't just give up my stuff, I gave up control of my life. I put the old man to death in order to live a fearless life with Christ:

> I have been crucified with Christ and I no longer live, but Christ lives in me. The life I now live in the body, I live by faith in the Son of God, who loved me and gave himself for me. (Gal. 2:20)

You ask, "Do you regret what you've lost?"

Lost? What are you talking about? There's not one thing I surrendered that wasn't joyfully given up. Remember, everything in my former life was eating away at my soul. No, I have no regrets:

> What is more, I consider everything a loss because of the surpassing worth of knowing Christ Jesus my Lord, for whose sake I have lost all things. I consider them garbage, that I may gain Christ. (Phil. 3:8)

Let me ask you what cancel culture is going to do to a guy like me. Slander me? Imprison me? Beat me? Kill me? Sorry, boys, I'm already a dead man. I've already heaped my stuff into an enormous pile and announced, "See this stuff? My reputation? My freedom? My life? Uh, it's all garbage."

I'm not saying it's not painful. In the moment, it can be (that's why it's called a sacrifice). But the promise of God is that, at some future date, on the other side of the resurrection (or maybe even on this side), we'll look back at death and taunt it. We'll mock sacrifice, persecution, and the grave:

Where, O death, is your victory?
Where, O Death, is your sting? (1 Cor. 15:55)

If you want to know why I'm still smiling after watching the cancel culture folks towering over believers, trying to intimidate them into submission, this is it. I have a friend on the inside who told me not to worry about it, that it'll all seem like nothing before too long. He's the one who instructed Paul to write, "For our light and momentary troubles are achieving for us an eternal glory that far outweighs them all" (2 Cor. 4:17). Imagine that! Paul, one of the most persecuted followers of Christ in the history of the church, reduced his mistreatment to "light and momentary troubles." He could say that because his eyes were focused on an eternal glory far greater than anything he had lost due to his belief in Jesus. Nope, no one can touch us when we follow Jesus even in death. Once we die to ourselves and bury the old people we were, we become one with him. The only thing I can tell anyone who wants to cancel me is this: "Have at it, but you're wasting your time! I've been inoculated. I was already canceled once, but the Almighty canceled my cancellation."

That's as good as it gets!

CHAPTER 7

JESUS CANCELS GUILT AND SHAME

Anyone who believes in him will
never be put to shame.
Romans 10:11

Thousands of people from all around the globe, young and old, black and white, doctors, lawyers, plumbers, college graduates, and high school dropouts all alike have walked through our door looking for something. Most of the time they didn't even know what they were looking for, but the one thing the majority of them had in common was the guilt and shame of a lifetime of sin weighing heavily on their hearts and minds. Most of them felt as if they had lost the power to exercise their free will and that their futures were carved in stone because of their pasts, because the consequences of their sin were stacked high on their consciences like cordwood.

The young women, after years of being objectified as sexual property by older males, had begun to show the physical strain of abuse in their faces. They looked older, more haggard than they should have. Some had been pregnant in their teens, others had lost children to child protective services, and others had aborted their unborn children. Many of the men had been victims of sexual and physical abuse and had fallen into drug and alcohol addictions, and now they struggled to achieve healthy relationships with women. Trust me when I tell you, we've seen it all. Searchers! All of them were searching. But for what? They usually didn't know.

And while their behaviors varied, they all looked the same to me. You could almost imagine they had neon signs dangling from their bowed necks: "I am guilty! If you knew only half of what I've done, you wouldn't love me. In fact, you wouldn't even speak to me." In their minds, these signs were perpetually shining as constant reminders of their worthlessness. The inner voice of guilt and shame said, *You are a failure! You are trash! You are guilty!*

It is a horrible cycle, to be sure. People have always had the tendency to be sinful. But ever since we told God to take a hike, one of the casualties is that we have lost the ability to navigate safely through life. As I've pointed out, the absence of God—even though he's not actually absent but ignored—means we are disconnected from truth and reality. Without someone greater than ourselves to guide our steps, we lose connection with the one reality that actually tells us what our true worth is. When we don't acknowledge that we bear the image of God, how can we find our actual value?

Perhaps the most devastating casualty of evicting God from our culture is that, without him, we have no path to redemption. In a godless world, once we've crossed the line, there is no way back. From that point on, we are defined in our minds and in the eyes of society by our sins. We tell ourselves, *I am a drug addict! I am a whore! I am an alcoholic! I am a failure at marriage! I am—* You get the point. Just fill in the blank with whatever negative image Satan has convinced you is true.

Once he has us defining ourselves by our sin, Satan proceeds to convince us that we are too far gone for God. "How could God love you after what you've done?" "Look at you! You're a mess!" "You are beyond hope."

But God created us with an ability to feel guilt and shame. They are designed to be warnings that we are on the wrong path, that we have wandered away from what will truly fulfil us, from the desire to know, love, and obey God our Father. But Satan? He's pretty good at hijacking what God intended for good and using guilt and shame to our detriment. Instead of guilt and shame warning us to turn around, the Evil One uses these gifts to convince us there is no turning back.

This is, by the way, the power source of cancel culture. Those who delight in canceling others prey upon our fear that our guilt and shame will be exposed in order to gain control over us. This is why God commands us to confess our sins openly. This has been my practice since I first became a follower of Jesus, and it's worked well for me. Once in a while someone will point out a salty social media headline that says something like "Phil Robertson Has Affair." My response is always the same. I laugh and say, "Well, duh! I already wrote about that in my book. That's old news!" This is one reason neither Satan nor the cancel culture crowd can hold anything over my head: I've already come clean about my past before the entire world. If you are living in fear that someone will really know the true version of yourself, how about you just obey God?

> Therefore, confess your sins to each other and pray for each other *so that you may be healed.* (James 5:16, emphasis added)

I am well aware of the inner voice that threatens us with cancellation if we publicly admit our sins, but that voice isn't ours. It only sounds like ours. It is the voice of the Evil One who knows how liberating public confession is. The last thing Satan wants us to do is admit our wrongdoing, because he knows once we come clean before others, he loses his power over us.

The problem is that once guilt and shame are used by the Evil One and by those doing his bidding, shame becomes our master. It takes our breath away and robs us of our rest. It is a heavy burden we carry twenty-four hours of every day. It nags us when we are awake and haunts us in our dreams. It prevents us from seeing that God has already provided a path out of the swamp that has become our lives.

When I think about the power of misguided guilt and shame to control us, I've often wondered why people ever come to Miss Kay and me in the first place. For some reason (I suspect it is a last-ditch stab in the dark) they journey through the planted pine thickets and swampy bayous to our house because they hope to find something, anything that will be a balm for their painful self-inflicted wounds that have begun to fester. By the time they wander into my house, all they can see is their moral rot and decay. They cannot, they dare not see themselves as image bearers of the Most High God. They want a little hope. Not much. Just enough to get them through the night. So they come with heads bowed low, barely able to even glance in my direction.

Most of them have heard my testimony and figured, *Hey, if the Almighty can save a filthy wretch like Phil Robertson, maybe there's hope for me.* I'm not proud of my former life, when I lived in open rebellion to the Almighty, but I'm not ashamed to tell the story because it is in the telling that others begin to grasp an important, indisputable fact: our God specializes in restoring beauty to those who have made themselves ugly by sin. These people are right. If God could save a man like me, just think what he can do with them. I say that because, before I met Jesus, I was at the bottom of the moral heap. When I ran into him, I was chin-deep in alcohol swigging, dope smoking, serial adultery, fornicating. Well, you get the point. There aren't many people worse than I was. You talk about guilt and shame! I was covered in it. I had plunged headlong into the Evil One's filthy pigsty and wallowed. I heaped handfuls of filth on my head and rubbed it in. I wanted to be clean, but it seemed impossible to me at the time. Still, despite my utter rejection of God and his law, he was willing to pour his mercy on me in abundance. No matter that I needed more than most people; he has more than an ample supply. He is the God of limitless mercy.

On the very worst day of my former life, two things were true. One, I was indeed hopeless, beyond redemption. At least that's what I thought. My religious upbringing did not allow for grace or mercy. In my youth, I was taught, even after giving my life to Christ, I would be immediately cut off as soon as I committed my next sin. The only way back was to repent and ask for mercy. But what if I were to die before I could utter a prayer? According to what I was told, I would be lost. This was a petri dish perfectly primed to cultivate a growth of shame. Shame can be a catalyst for repentance, but Satan's desire is to keep us trapped in the downward spiral of shame heaped upon shame. He convinces us there's no way out. But I have some good news for you: he lies!

The second thing that is true about the worst day of my former life is that God has never loved me more or less than he did on that day. He doesn't love me more now that I am his follower than he did on the day I was in complete rebellion against him. He may be more pleased with me now, but he doesn't love me more. He so loved me at my lowest that he gave his only Son as a sacrifice for my sin. He so loved me that his Son died in my place. You may be thinking, *How can that be? How can a holy God love someone who is shaking a fist in his face and making a declaration of independence from the authority of the God who created him?* The answer is that he is not only holy, he is also love: "So we know and rely on the love God has for us. God is love" (1 John 4:16). This passage doesn't say that God is loving but that he is love. So I realized at some point that God's love isn't just a concept or an idea but that it is who he is.

What does this have to do with cancel culture? It has

everything to do with cancel culture because cancel culture is an agent of Satan to convince you that you are unworthy and beyond redemption, that you have crossed the point of no return. Cancel culture's aim is to shame you into submission to its code, to shut you up. It wants to convince you that your past is permanently wrapped around your neck like a millstone. It weighs you down today, and it will still be weighing you down tomorrow, only more so. Its goal is to instill fear, shame, and debilitating guilt. It's like the lyric about checking out but never leaving, from the Eagles' song "Hotel California."

That's the goal of shame and perpetual guilt: you can never leave. You may not even be guilty of the things you are accused of, but you're guilty of something. So am I! Everyone is! So we are easy marks for the shame merchant, Satan! He wants to lock us up and throw away the key. But we don't need to be confused about his intentions.

While we are recognizing the evil intent of the devil, we also need to know that a far more powerful being is actually working for our good: our Lord and Savior, Jesus Christ. He is the remedy for hopeless shame and guilt because when he died on the cross, both guilt and shame were crucified with him:

> If you declare with your mouth, "Jesus is Lord," and believe in your heart that God raised him from the dead, you will be saved. For it is with your heart that you believe and are justified, and it is with your mouth that you profess your faith and are saved. As Scripture says, "Anyone who believes in him will never be put to shame." (Rom. 10:9–11)

If you are living in shame, you should read this verse every day for the next year because the secret—even though it's not a secret at all since God has revealed it—to overcoming overwhelming guilty feelings and the accompanying shame is right here. A person who is convinced that Jesus is, in fact, Lord and openly confesses his name *and* believes that Christ has literally been raised from the dead is immune to the sneaky misdeeds of Satan.

Since freedom from shame is closely linked to confessing that Jesus is Lord, what does that mean? The word *lord* applies to anyone who has complete dominion and control over another. It's that simple! To confess Jesus as Lord is to admit that you are incapable of guiding your own steps (as all of us have already demonstrated), but he is not only capable, he is the only one worthy to do so. When we admit that he alone is Lord, we relinquish control. We hand over our lives to him and trust he is able and willing to give us direction.

I don't like the word *formula* when it comes to talking about how we can stop the downward spiral of guilt and shame, but it'll have to do here. The second part of the formula is to believe in our hearts that Christ is risen from the dead. This might be the most important part of the formula because the resurrection of Christ from the dead means we can trust Jesus as Lord. Think about it. Why would anyone want to give control of their lives to a god who died only to stay dead? That kind of god is weak, powerless to do anything to eliminate our shame. Even if he had been an all-powerful god, we would never know it. An unrisen Christ would mean we would never know for sure if our sins had been dealt with. No one could argue, however, with the fact that a risen Christ can be trusted with the most valuable thing in our lives: our salvation from sin. Another way of saying that is, if the resurrection of Christ from the grave is a historical event, then his promise to never allow us to be put to shame can be trusted. You can be confident of that—if Christ has been raised.

I suppose this boils down to who you are going to trust: the accusations of the Evil One who accuses you of perpetual guilt, who tells you that you are beyond hope, or the promise of the one who was raised from the dead, the promise that tells you that all your guilt—past, present, and future—has been nailed to the cross, never to be remembered by God any longer.

This is why cancel culture is water off a duck's back so far as I'm concerned. While it is true I have a dark and ugly past, it is also true I've put my faith in the resurrected Son of God who died for me. He died to set me free from the law of sin and death. There's no room for shame in my heart. God's already taken that burden off my back and put it on his. Here's what I need to know: God knows me! There isn't one thing about me—no sin, no thought, no evil desire, no private moment that God isn't aware of. And guess what! Even though I am fully known by God, I am fully loved by him. Is that good news or what? Not only is it true about me, but it's true about you as well. God knows you like he knows the back of his mighty hand, and he still adores you. You are fully known and fully loved.

Let me ask you, Do you think you can find this kind of love anywhere else? No! There is no one else who will love you in the same way, unconditionally and in spite of all your warts and flaws. This is why I stand unashamed before cancel culture: God knows me and still loves me. I can stand before him without shame because he nailed my guilt to the cross. So if I'm able to stand before the Creator without shame, why would I care what another person says about me?

What, then, shall we say in response to these things? If God is for us, who can be against us? (Rom. 8:31)

CHAPTER 8

CHECK YOUR PASSPORT

*Jesus Cancels Addiction
to Worldly Systems*

But our citizenship is in heaven.
Philippians 3:20

Miss Kay? I'm pretty sure she never met a road she didn't like. Unlike me, she loves to travel. If she's not wearing out the tires on her Ford Expedition heading to a ladies' Bible study in town, she's using up those airline miles to visit friends and family. Our boys are just like her. Even when we were scraping out a living, trying to get our business off the ground, they were flying from one developing nation to another and spreading the good news of Jesus.

I've observed two things about their travels. One, they always comment on the stark contrast between the lives we live in the United States and how people live in other countries. Life can be hard when poverty and oppression are a way of life. Another thing I've noticed is that, even though they seem to enjoy their journeys, they can't wait to get back home. This country is amazing, I have to admit.

Trust me when I tell you that I love America. Never before in the history of mankind has any political system offered its citizens more freedom than ours does. For almost 250 years, we have been able to do as we please as long as we do not trample on the rights of others. Not only that, but we are known as the land of opportunity for a reason. Children born into poverty can rise up to possess wealth their parents never imagined possible. People from all around the globe see our nation for what it is: a place where the have-nots can become the haves.

That's why, in 2021, folks from Mexico and Central America

were pouring across our southern border by the hundreds of thousands, maybe even a million.[1] They were desperate for the opportunity to have what we have: a chance to rise out of poverty and live a decent life.

Yes, I love America. But I have to be honest with you, my hope for the future isn't wrapped up in the American flag. If our government imploded tomorrow and all of our freedoms were suddenly jerked from our grasp, I would mourn her death, but I would not wring my hands and throw in the towel. That's because I stand in the presence of God. I'm a free man who was bought and paid for by the mercy of God. And since he owns me, I am here only to obey him and glorify his name. When he bought me, I surrendered my old passport and voluntarily became a citizen of his kingdom:

> But our citizenship is in heaven. And we eagerly await a Savior from there, the Lord Jesus Christ, who, by the power that enables him to bring everything under his control, will transform our lowly bodies so that they will be like his glorious body. (Phil. 3:20–21)

The reason this is important is that I've been listening to people discuss politics as if our future depended on the outcome of every election. They say things such as, "Our Christian freedoms are being eroded." I'm told that many in the Christian community post scandalous, hateful, degrading memes about the opposition on social media. Some of my brethren have recently begun to advocate for a violent overthrow of the government.

Let me ask, Can you point to anything Jesus ever said or the apostles ever wrote that gave even a hint of obsession on their part about worldly governments? I ask that because I've looked, and I can't find it. The only thing Jesus said about government was, "Give back to Caesar what is Caesar's, and to God what is God's" (Matt. 22:21). Wasn't Caesar corrupt? Weren't his elections rigged? Weren't babies being killed and innocent people being executed? Did the average Roman citizen or the citizens of the empire have anything close to our Bill of Rights? Our First Amendment? Compared with the United States, would you say Rome was more or less evil? The truth is, the United States can't yet hold a candle to the corruption of first-century Rome, but the only thing Jesus had to say about the empire was, "Give back to Caesar what is Caesar's." Jesus seemed to have no obsession with the quality of a government at all.

Neither did the apostles. If God's purpose for his church was to straighten out the worldly systems of the first century, don't you think he would have said something about it in Scripture? This isn't to say we shouldn't get involved and do good when we can—we should. But the church should be a leavening influence on culture, including politics, and we are given specific instructions about how to accomplish that: "I urge, then, first of all, that petitions, prayers, intercession and thanksgiving be made for all people—for kings and all those in authority, that we may live peaceful and quiet lives in all godliness and holiness" (1 Tim. 2:1–2). Did you get that? We're talking about ushering in a revolution by praying and petitioning the Almighty to bring about political change.

And while we're at it, don't forget Romans 13:1–2: "Let everyone be subject to the governing authorities, for there is no authority except that which God has established. The authorities that exist have been established by God. Consequently, whoever rebels against the authority is rebelling against what God has instituted, and those who do so will bring judgment on themselves." I understand that this passage flies in the face of the revolutionary American spirit, but it says what it says. In my opinion, there's no ambiguity here. God is in charge.

Yes, work to change your culture, but turning things around could take hundreds of years. It was three hundred years between the day of Pentecost in Acts 2 and when Constantine made the Christian church legal. For most of that three hundred years, our early brothers and sisters were meeting in tombs and small rooms, hiding from the authorities. If it becomes illegal to worship God again, should I just wait until we get the government's approval before I can praise him? No. The advancing borders of God's kingdom do not wait on worldly systems.

I openly speak my mind about elections and social issues. I faithfully cast my vote. In fact, I'm usually one of the first to arrive at our polling place at Pinecrest School, which is not more than fifteen minutes from our house. Miss Kay and I usually make a date of it. But make no mistake about it, all of my hope is in Jesus and his kingdom, not in any political system, including the United States of America. This is not some kind of knee-jerk reaction to any recent election. I made the decision a long time ago to seek first his kingdom and his righteousness. I did so because Jesus promised me that when I make his kingdom my number-one priority, God will supply all of my needs, no matter how dire the political and social climate appears to be. "But seek first his kingdom and his righteousness, and all these things will be given to you as well" (Matt. 6:33). He's going to take care of me. So far, he hasn't let me down.

There's another reason I don't put too much hope in worldly systems: they all fail. This isn't just a logical response to the historical record, it is a truth that God revealed to the prophet Daniel when he told him that "he deposes kings and raises up others"

(Dan. 2:21). But the historical record is important here because it is littered with one mighty empire after another that was brought to its knees. From the Sumerians to the Babylonians to the Greeks to the Romans—they all collapsed. While Rome still exists today, it is a shell of its former glory, almost insignificant on the world stage. Same thing with Greece. I'm old enough to have witnessed the final days of the British Empire. Bit by bit it was dismantled, and England was left with only memories of its once glorious kingdom.

Empires all had two things in common: God wasn't at their center and they all collapsed. They rotted from the inside out. They were characterized by corruption and self-serving greed. They became callous to injustice.

I'm no prophet. I'm just an average guy, but I'm looking at America in the twenty-first century, and I'm seeing parallels to the ruins of the kingdoms of history. Greed, malice, slander, gossip (social media), hatred, discord, violence, murder, corruption, and so on. Could the United States be next? Is America on the brink of collapse? In my opinion, we are living off the capital of our godly founders. But how long will that last?

Of course, I have no answer to that question, but I don't think it's a stretch to say, at the very least, we are in trouble. Whether America survives or collapses, the only question I have about it is, What should our response be? As men and women of God, how should we react? My answer to these questions is exactly the same I would give you if you were to ask me how to respond to cancel culture: admit that you are a stranger and an alien here. While we speak out against injustice and for the fair treatment of our neighbors, we can't obsess about how the ungodly will respond.

As the writer of Hebrews said about the persecuted saints of

God's kingdom, "They were foreigners and strangers on earth" (11:13).

Think about that for a second. "Foreigners and strangers on earth"? On the few occasions I have traveled outside of the United States, I've noticed one thing: I don't have the same rights as the citizens of the countries I visit. I can't express my opinion about their government by voting in their elections. I can't take up residence there without getting permission to become a permanent resident. I am completely at the mercy of the systems that govern those countries. Bottom line? I don't really belong there! I am a stranger in a foreign land. My home is somewhere else, and by the end of my journey, I often found myself longing for that home, for my humble abode on the banks of the Ouachita River.

Accepting the fact that I'm a poor wayfaring stranger here means I am liberated from the obligation to put my trust in anything that offers no hope beyond the here and now. It also sparks a desire to be with God in his kingdom. Think about it. What if we were able to establish a perfect republic where there were no injustices? What if we could eliminate political corruption and greed? What if we could elect the perfect leader? What if we could destroy racism and bigotry? The bad news is, we can't. We are too weak and too sinful to accomplish it. But the good news is that the Almighty's kingdom is perfect in all of these areas. There is no corruption! No racism! No bigotry! No greed! And to top it all off, our leader is a holy, righteous, perfect, all-powerful, and loving God. We will never see that in our worldly leaders. Never. But we see it in our Father. Whatever injustices, whatever wrongs, whatever pain and sorrow we face in the here and now for the sake of God's kingdom, we must face it with one promise in mind:

"He will wipe every tear from their eyes. There will be no more death" or mourning or crying or pain, for the old order of things has passed away. (Rev. 21:4)

You talk about liberating! I confess that I don't always make a kingdom response to the events occurring around me, but when I am in the mode of daily reaffirming my commitment and love for the kingdom of God, I don't get too caught up in the affairs of the world. Why should I? The worldly leaders are driven by a different set of rules than I am. For example, I want to imitate Christ, who came not to be served, but to serve. In worldly systems, however, a servant leader is a rare bird. Politicians and kings are more preoccupied with amassing power and enriching themselves. And while I believe that kingdom mindedness has the power to transform the hearts and minds of the most cynical and callous political types, I also know power is intoxicating, an addictive drug that promises to enrich anyone who seeks it. The problem is that the lie never lives up to expectations. So when I tell you to start acting like you are a kingdom-driven follower of Christ, I am actually telling you to be liberated from the disappointing rules of worldly systems. Those systems promise liberty but always wind up putting us in bondage.

This is the perfect point to talk about another reason I'm not overly vested in worldly systems. While some political kingdoms can be powerful, all of them will be destroyed. There are no exceptions to this rule. All of them will collapse, including the greatest country in the history of the world: the United States of America. But the kingdom of God is different in that it is eternal. In other words, it existed before the foundation of the world, and it will exist long after the world has melted away. Ponder the following verse because it is the foundation of kingdom living:

> But the day of the Lord will come like a thief. The heavens will disappear with a roar; the elements will be destroyed by fire, and the earth and everything done in it will be laid bare.
>
> Since everything will be destroyed in this way, what kind of people ought you to be? You ought to live holy and godly lives as you look forward to the day of God and speed its coming. That day will bring about the destruction of the heavens by fire, and the elements will melt in the heat. But in keeping with his promise we are looking forward to a new heaven and a new earth, where righteousness dwells. (2 Peter 3:10–13)

Everything you can experience with your five senses is destined for annihilation. Every molecule, every atom, every cell of every living thing will be burned up. I call this, by the way, the ultimate global warming. Before this celestial meltdown occurs, however, it is possible my life will already have come to an end. Let's face it, friends, I'm in my midseventies. The truth is I don't have long to live on this planet. But the implication of this passage is that a better dwelling awaits me: a new creation where righteousness dwells. Like the apostle Peter, I am looking forward to that day. A day that signals the end of injustice, the end of unrighteousness, and the end of death. I'm not sad about it. In fact, I'm excited about *the new heaven and the new earth*.

To be honest with you, this realm in which we live is chock-full of disappointments. I'm not saying I don't experience joy and happiness here on earth. I do. But when I look around me, I see pain and suffering. Loved ones die. My own death is looming on the horizon. Divorce, abuse, injustice, addictions, hatred, unrest, gossip, slander, discord, and a whole host of other ugly sins continually hover almost everywhere I go. Sometimes I am weary, to be honest. So the promise of a restored creation, where I will dwell with God and all of that junk will be eradicated, permanently destroyed, well, it just creates an intense longing for me to be there.

Peter asked a great question in the above passage. If everything we think is important will be destroyed in the fervent heat of the end times, what kind of people should we be? Another way of asking the question is this: How should we live? Should we live as if the elements of the world will give our lives meaning and purpose? I don't think so, because living for molecules and atoms is foolish, since they will eventually evaporate. They are temporary. They won't last. What good will they do us then? The reason I am not in despair because of my age is that I have rejected the temporary in favor of the eternal, and everything is temporary on this side of the resurrection. Things, pain, disease, and death. We'll all look around one day and realize it's all on fire. You'll see the smoke spiraling into the heavens and realize you made an incredibly good decision to not let the temporary things of this world control your life. You will dance with joy that you did not give your allegiance to the systems of this world or to the people who run them. At that point, you will not regret that you turned control of your life over to the one who is eternal, the one who is good.

I'll speak up about culture and point out its flaws, but that's not my life. I live for the One who died for me and was raised on my behalf. I'm going with Jesus the rest of the way home. From where I sit, that is the slickest move I can make because, in his kingdom, everything is always flawlessly perfect.

CHAPTER 9

I AIN'T AFRAID OF NO GHOSTS!

Jesus Cancels the Fear of the Unknown

For God has not given us a spirit of fear and
timidity, but of power, love, and self-discipline.
2 Timothy I:7 NLT

A few years ago I was reclining in my easy chair on a rainy Saturday afternoon, alternating between Fox News, the History Channel, and the Weather Channel. Simultaneously and with no warning at all, Miss Kay's two rat terriers, JJ and Jesse, sounded the alarm that someone was about to enter through the kitchen door. JJ and Jesse have since gone on to the doghouse in the sky, but I'll say this for them: when it came to announcing visitors, they never got it wrong—not one false alarm. They were good at their job, no question about it.

Just as the dogs approached the door, it swung open and in sauntered one of those river-rat church brothers I used to hang around with. He barged in like he lived here, and to be honest, our home had an open-door policy. Early on in our walk with Christ, we made hospitality our practice. We still do.

On the heels of my church brother was an even seedier-looking redneck who appeared as if he'd been on a three-week drinking binge.

From the comfort of my recliner, I called out, "Come on in, boys. Y'all hungry?" One thing I've discovered over the years is that I've never met a redneck who wasn't hungry.

My church brother got right to the point. He pointed his thumb toward his friend and said, "Junior here's got a serious drinking problem, and I told him you'd tell him about Jesus."

One look at the dude and I knew two things. First, no one had to tell me he had a drinking problem. He reeked of cheap alcohol. His eyes were bloodshot and weary. No doubt about it, he had more than a drinking problem; he was a full-blown alcoholic. Second, nobody ever had to ask me twice to share the gospel of Jesus. That's what I lived for then, and it's what I live for now.

But before I got into a Bible study with the young drunk, I fed the boy. He looked like he hadn't eaten in a week or two.

As soon as we finished eating, I opened my large-print Thompson Chain-Reference Bible (the one held together with duct tape) and began to preach Jesus to him. Everything went fine until I got to the point about Jesus being our way out of the grave. Believe me when I tell you that it's very difficult to shock me, but this fellow left me speechless by what he said.

I had given him my standard, "Everybody's headed to a six-foot hole in the ground. What's your plan for escaping it?"

"I'm not going to die!" he said angrily through gritted teeth as if he really meant it.

I waited a few seconds for him to crack a smile and let me in on the joke. Unfortunately, he was dead serious.

"Oh, everybody's going to die, son, trust me on this one. You are no exception," I replied.

The young man's face shaded beet red, his shoulders hunched, his fists clenched involuntarily, and he began to quiver. As he rose angrily from the well-worn couch, I braced myself for a sucker punch.

"Nobody's gonna tell me I'm gonna die! Nobody!" he said and stomped out the door, slamming it behind him. That was the end of it. Sadly, I never saw him again.

A few weeks later, the church brother was back at the house. As he dropped his oversized frame onto the couch, he said, "Hey, you remember that dude? Junior? The one who said he would never die? You're not going to believe this. He got in a bar fight last night and was stabbed to death."

To tell you the truth, that was one of the saddest days of my life. This young man, barely old enough to legally drink, had embraced a lie so deadly, so deceptive, that it cost him his life. I didn't know him well enough to say for sure, but it's been my experience that people (including yours truly) who excessively use alcohol and illicit drugs are trying to compensate for their confusion about the realities of life, about how uncertain and fleeting it is. Now in my midseventies, I can tell you that my life has been a flash in the pan. Only yesterday I was a quarterback in front of thousands of fans at Joe Aillet Stadium on Louisiana Tech's campus. All of mine and Miss Kay's needs were met by adoring football fans simply because they valued my ability to throw a football. I thought it would last forever. It pains me to tell you that I am now officially an old man. Believe me when I tell you I am shocked at how fast my life has sped by me.

Yes, life is short. The Bible says it's a "mist that appears for a little while and then vanishes" (James 4:14). You see it for a second or two, then it's gone forever. We don't like to think too much about it, but we all know that the infamous six-foot hole awaits us. They'll lower my dead body into one, and they'll do the same for yours. Admittedly, we don't like the idea. In fact, most of us have a quivering fear of death, a paralyzing fear.

I suppose a great deal of our fear of death stems from the fact that we were created to live forever (Gen. 1–3). We are, by nature, eternal beings. Eternity is written on our hearts (Eccl. 3:11). Unfortunately, our ancestors rebelled against God, and a death sentence was pronounced on them and us. Now, everyone dies (Heb. 9:27). We can spend hours in the gym in a vain effort to recapture our youthful bodies or we can submit ourselves to a plastic surgeon and create the illusion we are young, but trust me when I tell you that we are fighting a losing battle. We still die. You will die and so will I.

While we may be uncomfortable thinking about it, we know deep down in our souls that it's a fact. As I said, a six-foot hole awaits us all. Every last one of us.

Yes, I know that sounds morbid. It not only sounds morbid, it is morbid. Death goes against our nature. We were created in the image of an eternal God, and because we bear his image, we were destined for eternal life. That's why we fear death. That's why it confuses us! It's not supposed to be like this.

That's also why the young man I told you about was so angry. He couldn't contemplate a time when he wouldn't exist. He knew he mattered, he just didn't know why, and not knowing why cost him his life.

What I wish he could have known is that he bore God's image. He mattered for that reason alone. I wish he could have known that the Creator of the cosmos loved him immeasurably. I wish that he could have known this God died in his stead and was raised from the grave so he wouldn't have to fear death. I wish that he could have known the God who raised Jesus' lifeless body from the tomb also promised to raise him up and give him a new and perfect resurrection body. Yes, I wish that he could have turned off his filter for a moment and heard the good news about Jesus! If he had, he would not have been angry with the message but would have fallen on his knees before our God and repented of his sins. He would have openly and loudly confessed that Jesus is Lord. He would have had God's mercy wash over him like a river and cleanse his heart from all unrighteousness, and he would have had his fear of death washed away with it. Ignoring the reality of death did him no good at all. He would have been better off to have faced it and prepared for it:

> Since the children have flesh and blood, he too shared in their humanity so that by his death he might break the power of him who holds the power of death—that is, the devil—and free those who all their lives were held in slavery by their fear of death. (Heb. 2:14–15)

That is gospel, right there. Christ became one of us when he inhabited human flesh. When he died, he destroyed Satan's power to dangle the threat of death over our heads. The devil steals our joy by reminding us that we don't have long, then he turns around and convinces us that we shouldn't think about our own mortality. "Go find a distraction," he commands us. "Find a counterfeit. Just don't think about the brevity of your life."

C. S. Lewis said it perfectly:

> It would seem that Our Lord finds our desires not too strong, but too weak. We are half-hearted creatures, fooling about with drink and sex and ambition when infinite joy is offered us, like an ignorant child who wants to go on making mud pies in a slum because he cannot imagine what is meant by the offer of a holiday at the sea. We are far too easily pleased.[1]

Indeed, we are too easily pleased. Ambition, drink, and illicit sex are poor substitutes for the infinite joy we can have when we seek the Lord. I'm looking at the folks who run after these things (remembering when they were a priority to me too), and I don't see infinite joy. They settled for less, as did I. The sad truth is that the joy of sin lasts only until the bottle of whiskey runs dry. Sex brings ecstatic joy that lasts only a few seconds after the climax. The joy of wealth is temporary in the same way. All of these diversions make us feel happy for a moment, but we always need more. They always leave us wanting. That's because they do not offer any hope beyond the moment. At the end of the sexual encounter or the influx of cash or the night out on the town, we still haven't answered the most important question of all: How do I get this body out of the grave? When the dust settles, we are still destined for the hole in the ground.

Let's be honest. Running after counterfeits only heightens our sense that life is brief and that we don't matter. Am I right? After it's over, don't you still feel empty and hopeless? More hopeless than you were before? Sin makes big promises but never delivers. In fact, we always wind up with less than we had to begin with. It diminishes. It is a thief that steals joy, purpose, and meaning.

This is why the threat of being canceled is so powerful. We fear losing what little we have: our reputations, our careers, our sense of belonging to a community. When we offend the sensitivities of the cancel culture mind, it rises up in false indignation and threatens to destroy what we have. It threatens to diminish our lives, and it scares us.

But the passage above from Hebrews should encourage us when we discover our Lord died in our place so that Satan could no longer dangle the threat of death over our heads as the ultimate form of cancellation. While I've observed that people who don't get Jesus live in sheer terror of taking their last breath, those who follow Christ live bold, purposeful, joyful lives. It's not that death doesn't concern them or that they enjoy the thought of it, but their confidence in the work of Christ on the cross overpowers their fear. They live confidently because they've had the question of how they're going to get out of the grave answered. They've put their faith in Jesus.

When you answer that question—the one about how you are going to recover from death—you won't believe the surge of power you'll experience that will enable you to live boldly and fearlessly. If you want a biblical example of what I'm talking about, read about Stephen the deacon (Acts 6:8–7:60). The Jewish leaders had trumped up charges against Stephen and brought him before the Jewish court, where they would decide his fate. This group of so-called religious men held the power of life and death over Stephen.

You may have contemplated a question such as "What would I do if I were dragged before a federal court where the judge and jury were Christ haters, and I was required to answer for my faith in Jesus? What would I do? Would I cower or stand firm as I inspected the courtroom and saw the angry mob? Would I wilt at the sight of the lethal-injection table in the corner?" Our understanding of what Christ did when he died and was raised from the dead will determine how we answer that question. If your Christianity is cultural, if you are simply a church member only because your parents or spouse are church members, then you would probably renounce your faith. If that describes you, you have no basis for standing firm and proclaiming the name of Jesus before your accusers. Why would you? To you, he was just a fair-skinned man with long hair, like the Jesus depicted in the paintings of the Renaissance. Your savior is just a lamb-petting nice guy.

But if the Jesus you know is the Jesus from the Gospels, that's another matter altogether. He is a man of deep conviction. He is willing to put his life in danger in order to proclaim the kingdom of God. He is capable of the wrath that ripped apart the money-changers' booths outside the temple. But even more than that, he is a fierce lion whose resurrected body evoked fear in the apostle John. In John's encounter (Rev. 1:9–20), Jesus' appearance was a far cry from the paintings of the 1300s. His voice was so intense it drove John to his knees. After his death and resurrection, he was an imposing figure, otherworldly. The eyes of Jesus glowed with fire as did his feet. Dressed in a long white robe with a golden sash around his chest, a double-edged sword protruded from his mouth. His voice sounded like the thunder of rushing waters. He had just won the biggest fight in the history of the universe: he had conquered death.

The being who stood before John was intimidating, so intimidating that John could only do one thing: he fell on his face. Read the first chapter of the book of Revelation. This is not the Jesus of the cultural Christian church. You can't be passive about this Jesus. When this is the Jesus you worship, you don't fear death—you fear him. That is, you fear him until you realize he is on the side of all who worship him. He's your personal warrior who can defeat not only your opponents but death itself. In fact, he had already defeated death when he was raised from the grave.

It was this Jesus that Stephen was on trial for preaching about in Acts 6–7. Had he preached a Jesus more like the one preached in many churches today, Stephen would have been given a pass. A Jesus like that poses no threat to anyone. But the religious leaders knew that anyone who followed the Christ proclaimed by Stephen would reject their leadership. After all, who wants to follow flawed preachers and politicians when a mighty, all-powerful God in human flesh is standing before them?

So what did Stephen do? After a lengthy sermon, he concluded:

You stiff-necked people! Your hearts and ears are still uncir-
cumcised. You are just like your ancestors: You always resist
the Holy Spirit! Was there ever a prophet your ancestors did not
persecute? They even killed those who predicted the coming of
the Righteous One. And now you have betrayed and murdered
him—you who have received the law that was given through
angels but have not obeyed it. (Acts 7:51–53)

These are hardly the words of a man intimidated by calculating politicians, the cancel culture of the first century. In fact,
these are the words of either a lunatic or someone who knew the
Jesus that John saw in Revelation. This is a man who had full
confidence that regardless of what the Jewish leaders did to him,
God would make him victorious in the end, when he raised his
lifeless body from the grave.

As it turned out, the response of the religious zealots was
exactly what you would expect from the cancel culture crowd:

When the members of the Sanhedrin heard this, they were furi-
ous and gnashed their teeth at him. But Stephen, full of the
Holy Spirit, looked up to heaven and saw the glory of God,
and Jesus standing at the right hand of God. "Look," he said,
"I see heaven open and the Son of Man standing at the right
hand of God."

At this they covered their ears and, yelling at the top of
their voices, they all rushed at him, dragged him out of the city
and began to stone him. (vv. 54–58)

Look, these people have the power to do considerable harm
to us. I'll give them that. But it's only considerable harm if Jesus
is still in the tomb. If he was indeed raised from the dead, then we

can have full confidence that his promises are valid and that he has every intention of keeping them. In a very real sense, death is a temporary condition for those who follow the resurrected Lord Jesus. We don't have to be confused about this at all. Nor should we fear it.

CHAPTER 10

THE PERFECT GPS

Jesus Cancels Confusion

I have been crucified with Christ and I no
longer live, but Christ lives in me.
Galatians 2:20

Have you ever been lost in the woods? I mean, like you had no idea where you were or which direction was which? Someone asked me recently if I'd ever lost my way in the woods. I said, "I've never been lost, but I've been turned around for two or three days!"

Being lost in the wilderness is bad; it can even be dangerous. During the days when I would sometimes get turned around, I would examine my surroundings to see if I could make sense of them. Admittedly, I was usually up to no good in those days, so getting turned around was a natural consequence of my lifestyle. But whenever I did get lost, I would ask myself, *Where is north? If I can find north, I can find east.* But when the clouds obscure the sun, and neither sun, moon, nor stars are visible, finding one's bearings is impossible. More than once I would act on impulse, relying on my instincts. You might ask, "How did that work out for you, Phil?"

You already know the answer to that question. Relying on instinct made me even more lost than I had been when I started. The truth is, I needed something or someone of substance, someone greater or more knowledgeable than I, to guide me. I needed someone who knew the way. I needed a celestial marker to help me get my bearings. When we are on our own, we finally realize we have no idea where we are or how we are going to find our way home, and panic begins to creep in like a slow-rising tide. Soon that panic tries to act as our guide and compels us to run headlong in one direction or another, not caring whether we are headed the right way or not. We are just hoping, at that point, that we will sooner or later wind up in a familiar place.

It's bad enough to get lost in the woods, but it's much worse when someone loses their way spiritually, when they are disconnected from the God who not only made them but loves them. And if I could think of one word to describe America in the twenty-first century, it would be *lost*. Maybe there are other words that would work just as well: *off course, astray, disoriented*. How about the word *confused*? Does that describe what it's like to live without God? When we don't know him and we are attacked, don't our minds cloud with confusion? Whatever word you choose to sum up our culture today, it would have to be one that correctly describes a people who have no moral compass, who not only lack a sense of direction back home but don't even know there is a home. We are unaware of our lostness, unaware that we've been turned around for a while.

I'm not trying to beat a dead horse, but this is exactly what happens when people as a group abandon God. When they don't "think it worthwhile to retain the knowledge of God" (Rom. 1:28). You ask, "Is America confused?" All I can say is I've never seen *so much* confusion!

Don't misunderstand me. I'm not sitting within the safe confines of my simple home and gleefully pronouncing judgment on America. I'm a God follower, and the God I follow says, "I take no pleasure in the death of anyone, declares the Sovereign LORD. Repent and live!" (Ezek. 18:32). Neither do I take pleasure when others rebel against God. It torments me. The truth is, I'm in the warning business. I try to point lost people to the only reliable moral compass there is: Jesus Christ. Almost every day I am begging folks to repent, to turn around and run after God. I'm begging people to choose life.

The good news is that many do. But sadly some choose not to. Still, I press on because, at one point in my life, someone pressed on with me even though, by all appearances, I had no interest in hearing about the God who died and was raised for me. But they kept at it, a relentless attack on the falsehoods that had become my worldview and had prevented me from living the abundant life.

Was I confused at the time? Ha! What are you talking about? I thought, because I had believed the lies, I could find no ful-fillment in a monogamous relationship with my wife. It never occurred to me I would find joy in leading my boys into manhood. I was repulsed by any suggestion that I could be encouraged by assembling with brothers and sisters in worship and Bible study. The truth is, my life was characterized by moral and spiritual confusion. I was, well, I was bewildered, filled with doubt and uncertainty, and perplexed. In other words, I was lost, turned around.

I find it ironic now, and I'm a little ashamed to admit it, but when I encountered anyone who loved me enough to point me to the One who could change my bewilderment into coherence, my doubt into confidence, and my confusion into certainty, I ran away from them. And when I was cornered and could not escape, I resorted to ridicule.

Did I know I was lost? Well, I can tell you that I knew I was one miserable rascal. You might ask, "How could you live like that, Phil?" The answer is that the only way I could endure the feelings of fear and panic that resulted from being turned around was to numb the pain with drugs, alcohol, and sex. Those were the big three diversions for me. The problem is, my diversions only exacerbated my feelings of confusion, the natural symptom of my lostness. As I understood it then, my only choice was to do more drugs, drink more alcohol, and sleep with more women. If I could talk to twenty-eight-year-old Phil, I would ask, "How do you think this is going to turn out? Do you really think this is going to work? Let me tell you about the one who loves you. Let me tell you about the one who died in your place!"

I've said a thousand times or more I wish I knew then what I know now. Another bad dude who regretted the choices he made in his youth was the man who would later become the apostle Paul. If you read the story of Stephen in the last chapter, you will have noticed something interesting in Acts 7:58. It's almost like Luke, the author of the book of Acts, just slipped it in to see if we would pick up on it: "the witnesses [to Stephen's stoning] laid their coats at the feet of a young man named Saul."

Saul? Who in the world is Saul? The answer is that he was the one commissioned by the Jewish leaders to ferret out everyone suspected of being a follower of this false teacher Jesus. The eighth chapter of Acts begins with the consequences of Stephen's execution, that is, it set the cancel culture of AD 36 on fire. Verse 1 says, "On that day"—only two or three years after Jesus had been crucified—"a great persecution broke out against the church in Jerusalem." And then "Saul began to destroy the church. Going from house to house, he dragged off both men and women and put them in prison" (v. 3).

Like me, Saul was confused. He was lost. He was turned around for a while. He lacked a moral compass. Even though he had the approval and blessing of Judea's religious leaders and teachers, he had no clue he was actually running full steam away from the one who could calm the raging fears of lostness that fueled his passion for canceling others.

Trust me when I tell you that today there is a mighty throng of people just like Saul. They may be male or female or speak English instead of Greek or Aramaic, but they are here by the millions. If they had the power to drag you off and throw your poor hide into prison, they would do it. Instead, they settle for destroying you, for getting you fired or disqualified for admission to the college you want to attend. They control governments and media. They are powerful members of college faculties. Sometimes they are living in their parents' basements and spending their time online looking for someone to devour. But make no mistake about it: they are here, and they are legion.

This may shock you, but the story of Saul actually helped to erase the confusion that had come to be my view of life. Until my eyes were opened, I assumed I was over the limit, my tab with God was too large to pay. Then I read about Saul. You might wonder, *How can a story of a violent persecutor of Christians be the story that gave you hope?*

Saul's story gave me hope because, in Acts 6–8, Saul had not yet come face-to-face with the risen Lord Jesus. He was still lost, still confused, still turned around for a time. It never occurred to most of the Christians of Saul's day that there was any hope that Saul's whacked-up view of reality could ever be corrected. They never imagined Saul would one day preach the same Jesus he persecuted other people for preaching.

But that is exactly what happened. Acts 9:1 says, "Meanwhile, Saul was breathing out murderous threats against the Lord's disciples." Within a day or two, Saul's confused, lost, bewildered life thankfully came to an end. What happened to him? He had

141

an encounter with the resurrected Jesus whom he had been per-secuting all this time. On his way to Damascus to put believers in jail, he ran smack dab into Jesus, or should I say Jesus ran headlong into Saul.

You should read the ninth chapter of Acts, but suffice it to say, Saul's hatred for all things Christian came to a screeching halt when he met Christ. It took less than a second for Saul to die. Of course, he didn't physically die at that point, but he died in the sense that the old Saul died. And the transformation that took place in his life was so profound that his name became Paul. Same body, same looks, same voice, but the old Saul was dead, and the man who arose was Paul.

In all probability I don't know you. There's a good chance we will never meet, but I do know one thing about you. No matter what you've done, no matter how sinful you've been, regardless of whether you have given Christians a hard time for their faith in Jesus, you aren't hopeless. If it's a new life you want, it's as available to you as it was to Saul the persecutor. For that matter, it's as accessible to you as it was to me.

Not long after I first put my faith in Christ and was baptized, I found the house Miss Kay and I still live in to this day. It is far off the beaten path, to say the least. I wanted it that way. For one, it sits just yards out of the floodplain of the Ouachita River. It is the perfect place to realize my goal of setting up my business of manufacturing and selling duck calls. But more important, it is so far from civilization that it would have been difficult for my old drinking buddies to find me. I already discussed this in my book *The Theft of America's Soul*, but I had been too easily persuaded by the self-professed atheist Al Bolen and his gang of misfits to join in their debauchery and drunkenness. I needed as much dis-tance from them as I could find.

But alas, find me they did. A year later they pulled into my yard and slithered like snakes from Al's vehicle.

"Robertson, we thought we'd never find you. We're here to party." The guys were toting in cases of beer and other fine beverages.

I'll admit I was a little nervous. All I knew to do was to give them a little testimony.

"Nah, boys, I'm not going to do that," I said. "I've put my faith in Jesus, and I live for him. Getting drunk is the last thing you'll find me doing."

My friend Al smirked and said, "Hey, Robertson, you on some kind of religious kick?"

It was a few seconds before I responded, but I'd been reading the story of how Saul became Paul. I'd been studying what Paul wrote about crucifying the old man and rising up from the grave of baptism to live a new God-gifted life. I'd been reading verses such as Galatians 2:20, "I have been crucified with Christ and I no longer live, but Christ lives in me."

To this day, I don't know where my response came from, but it shocked not only Al and the boys but me as well.

"Boys, I know y'all are looking for your old drinking partner, Phil Robertson," I told them, "but he died about a year ago. He's no longer alive. I have replaced him. I am the new Phil. The old one is dead. So you can stop searching for him. Christ has made a new man out of me."

Slowly they walked back to their muddy rig and drove away. It was years before I saw Al again. This time he was a humbled man. His prognosis from the doctor was not good. When he called and asked me to spend the day with him, I gladly retrieved my Bible from beside my recliner and drove to his house. I shared the story of Jesus with old Al and baptized him. Not long after that he breathed his last and was laid to rest. One of the greatest honors of my life was that his family asked me to preach at his funeral. When I told the people that day the story of Al's conversion to Jesus, there wasn't a dry eye in the place. They all knew what a scoundrel Al had been and saw his conversion for what it was—a miracle.

This is why Saul's conversion on the road to Damascus was so important in my conversion and in my development as a Christian. Initially, I figured, *If God can save a man like Paul, he can save me. If he can rescue Saul from being turned around in the wilderness, he can certainly rescue me.* Al came to the same conclusion about himself. He said, "If God can save a wretched adulterer, drug user, and drunk like Phil, he can save me too." When Al came face-to-face with Jesus on his own road to Damascus, he fell down before the Creator and Savior of the world. He admitted his open rebellion to God's authority, repented of his sins, put the old Al to death, and confessed that Jesus is Lord. Al came to Christ the same way Saul did, and he came to Christ the same way I did: empty-handed, bankrupt, and broken. And just like Saul and myself, God healed Al from the disease of moral confusion. Everything cleared up for Al in a split-second. I'm glad to report Al lived that way until he went to be with the Lord.

Let me add something here. I'm not claiming I am morally or intellectually superior to anyone else. On the contrary, I'm saying that whatever progress I've made in moving from confusion to clarity has been a work that God has done in me by the power of his Spirit. It's not about me but about the God who lives in me. And I suppose that is my point here. We are ill equipped to handle the onslaught of negativity on our own. When cancel culture attacks a person who is living in confusion, it only adds to the moral and emotional fog. But when a person who has the Spirit of the living God in their hearts is barraged with persecution, he or she sees it for what it is: Satan trying to use confused people to cancel out God by canceling us. He wants to destroy our passion for proclaiming that God is the God who gives clarity to those who are turned around. His goal is to demoralize us.

This is why we must be certain of two things: who we are, and who God is and what he has done for us. We were broken, sinful people who had no hope of clarity or redemption until we came into contact with Christ. We must be certain that God is holy and righteous and happens to love us so much that he gave his Son to pay the penalty for our sin.

Believe me when I tell you, when you internalize those two realities, no person who opposes you can do you permanent harm because you no longer live in a state of confusion. You are walking every step on a path illuminated by the Light of the World. You are walking with Jesus.

CHAPTER 11

WHO ARE YOU TO TELL ME WHAT TO DO?

Jesus Cancels False Morality

The law of the LORD is perfect,
refreshing the soul.
The statutes of the LORD are trustworthy,
making wise the simple.
Psalm 19:7

At the ripe old age of twenty-two years, Jerry Lee Lewis was at the pinnacle of his rockabilly career when he married Myra Brown. The problem was, she was his thirteen-year-old cousin. When the news broke, he was on tour in England. After only three performances, the rest of his performances were canceled. The scandal eventually drove Lewis's career into the ground.[1]

Only a few years earlier, actress Ingrid Bergman was one of the most influential women in the 1940s in Hollywood. Well, that is, until her affair with Roberto Rossellini and her unwed pregnancy became news in 1950. The uproar from the US press and the public was so great she lived in Europe for several years. If you're wondering how loud the uproar was over Bergman's sin, Colorado senator Edwin C. Jackson denounced her on the floor of the US Senate as a "powerful influence for evil."[2]

I won't argue that Lewis's and Bergman's actions were morally upright. Some might even argue these two celebrities got what they deserved, but I wouldn't personally make that argument. That's because I'm aware that, had I received what I deserved, I would have been struck dead on the spot. I'm sure not going to wish that on anyone. But one thing I've discovered over the years is that sin always has consequences. I've mentioned this before, but even after four and a half decades of being a Christian, sometimes something from my past pops up that reminds me that I rebelled against God too. It normally appears in an online article, and the headline makes it sound as if an investigative reporter has just uncovered some deep, dark secret from my past. I usually chuckle when I see these steamy headlines because the news isn't really news at all. Most of the time, I have already publicly admitted the sin they have just discovered. One thing is true, however; the headlines usually have a bit of truth in them.[3]

For some people, canceling others by sin-shaming is a way of life. They seem to enjoy it. People have been doing it to one another for as long as there have been people on this planet. The reason cancellation is so potent is that most people fear public exposure. It is this fear that fuels the engine of cancel culture. If no one cared about what was being said about them, cancel culture would abandon the effort and move on to something else. But we do care, and now that we have the power of the internet, it's like America has become a nonstop episode of *The Jerry Springer Show*, even a way of life.

The world is going to do what the world is going to do. As a follower of Jesus, however, I am compelled to ask myself, *Is that how Jesus handled the moral failures of others?* Did he attack the sexually immoral or the drunkards of his day? No, he did not. If the only thing you know about Christ is what you see in the lives of the Christians in your community, you may be surprised to find out that Jesus' regular practice was to defend the accused. You'll hear me say this a thousand times if you listen long enough: Jesus didn't come to heap shame and guilt on folks but to remove it.

The best example of Jesus' desire to defend the powerless is found in the eighth chapter of John's gospel. During one of Jesus' early morning Bible studies, a group of religious leaders paraded a woman who had been "caught in the act of adultery" through the streets of Jerusalem (v. 4). They forced her to stand (she was probably half-naked) before Jesus. Let that sink in for a moment. They caught her "in the act." They "forced" her to stand amid a crowd. You talk about sin-shaming. A sin she had hoped would remain hidden had been witnessed firsthand by a group of pastors. Now everyone knew about her sin. I'm sad to say, but God's pastors and teachers didn't care one bit about this woman; their only goal was to trap Jesus in a scriptural and moral dilemma by using her and her sin as bait. Either he would adhere to the letter of the Mosaic law and condemn her or he would show the compassion he was known for. He couldn't do both, they reasoned. Either way, they believed they had him cornered:

> The teachers of the law and the Pharisees brought in a woman caught in adultery. They made her stand before the group and said to Jesus, "Teacher, this woman was caught in the act of adultery. In the Law Moses commanded us to stone such women. Now what do you say?" They were using this question as a trap, in order to have a basis for accusing him. (vv. 3–6)

As it turns out, the Pharisees and teachers of the Law were only half right. Here's what the Mosaic law actually says:

> If a man is found sleeping with another man's wife, both the man who slept with her and the woman must die. (Deut. 22:22)

Jesus could have responded by saying, "You are correct! But where's the dude? Did she commit adultery all by herself? I don't think so! Now go get the other half of this sinful relationship and get back to me!" Even though he could have gone to Scripture to make his point, Jesus chose not to do so. Clearly, the woman was guilty of sin, and the religious leaders were right that she should be punished. She had, after all, violated the Law. Instead of condemning her, though, Jesus appealed to a higher law that truly reflects the nature and character of God's heart for sinners. He uncanceled her by reminding her accusers that they were guilty of sin too. Think about it: sinful lawbreakers demanding that a sinful lawbreaker be punished for her sin. That's what they did. But instead of joining the angry throng of her accusers, Jesus humiliated the humiliators:

> But Jesus bent down and started to write on the ground with his finger. When they kept on questioning him, he straightened up and said to them, "Let any one of you who is without sin be the first to throw a stone at her." Again he stooped down and wrote on the ground. (vv. 6–8)

This is one problem with cancel culture: condemnation appears to make an appeal to a compelling moral law. In the case of the woman caught in the act of sleeping with someone who was not her husband, it was God's law they appealed to. But the problem with moral laws is that no one keeps them all perfectly. Not even God's law. I'm not saying the law is evil, especially God's law. I've made the point for years that the Ten Commandments are the perfect law to keep a whole nation safe from harm. Just think, if everyone obeyed the Ten Commandments, what would America look like? I'll tell you: we would have a nation free of murder, larceny, rape, and divorce. We would certainly not have a cancel culture, since the Ten Commandments prohibit bearing false witness.

But who keeps the Law perfectly? You may have never committed adultery, but have you lied about others? Have you ever coveted a neighbor's success or possessions? Have you ever said, "I may have told a lie or two, but I've never murdered anyone"? When we say things like this, we think it somehow absolves us of most of our guilt. Yet when we say it, we are admitting we are sinners, admitting we are lawbreakers. This is how Jesus flipped the Pharisees' plan to trap him back on them. As it turned out, they trapped themselves because Jesus tied them up in a knot of their own lawlessness. No one is guilt-free, and the Pharisees and teachers of the Law immediately understood Jesus' point: "Go ahead and throw a stone if you are free from sin yourself!" Perhaps none of them were guilty of adultery, but they were all guilty of something, *and they knew it*!

> At this, those who heard began to go away one at a time, the older ones first, until only Jesus was left, with the woman still standing there. Jesus straightened up and asked her, "Woman, where are they? Has no one condemned you?"
>
> "No one, sir," she said.
>
> "Then neither do I condemn you," Jesus declared. "Go now and leave your life of sin." (vv. 9–11)

Did Jesus excuse the woman's adultery? No, he didn't, not even a little bit. He did not excuse her, but he did pardon her. He didn't cancel her, but he did cancel the debt she owed. He canceled her guilt and shame. As I've previously mentioned, if anyone ever had the right to condemn this woman and cancel her and banish her from Jewish society, it would have been Jesus. As the Creator of the cosmos and the author of the Law, he would have been completely justified in canceling her. In fact, had he retrieved a large rock from the ground and bashed in her head, he would have been right to do so. But that's not what he did. Instead, he forgave her! He redeemed her! He gave her a fresh start. And do you know why he did that? He did it because his love for her was greater than his desire to punish her. Why would he cancel someone he loved enough to die for? Jesus had the authority to condemn her but chose not to. The Pharisees did not have the authority to cancel her, but they tried.

Even though the Pharisees appeared to be appealing to the authority of Scripture, they were actually tweaking the Law to suit their own purposes. They didn't love God's Word as a message from the Almighty. Instead, they saw the situation as an opportunity to weaponize the Bible for their own purposes. The law of the Lord is perfect, but when we sift it to say what we want it to say to suit our own order of business, it is no longer the law of the Lord. It becomes a new law that does not have the power to revive the soul. The law of God is steadfast, but when we tinker with it, it ceases to be God's law. It becomes as shifty as any other code of law.

This is why we should be careful about passing judgment on anyone else, even if they are guilty. I meditate on the second chapter of Romans because it reminds me that I have no business, no right, to sit in the judgment seat due to the fact that I am as filthy as the next person:

> You, therefore, have no excuse, you who pass judgment on someone else, for at whatever point you judge another, you are condemning yourself, because you who pass judgment do the same things. Now we know that God's judgment against those who do such things is based on truth. So when you, a mere human being, pass judgment on them and yet do the same things, do you think you will escape God's judgment? Or do you show contempt for the riches of his kindness, forbearance and patience, not realizing that God's kindness is intended to lead you to repentance? (vv. 1–4)

Did you get that? If not, you should read it again because the consequences of missing this little nugget of spiritual truth can be catastrophic for you. Paul was saying that when you and I sit in the judgement seat—which is reserved for only one being, the Lord God Almighty—we are actually condemning ourselves. We are encouraged to judge behaviors, but pointing out sin is not what Paul was talking about here. The gist of this passage is that when we judge others in a way that elevates us and degrades others, we are bringing judgment on ourselves.

Just in case we missed his point, he made clear that judging others in a way that demoralizes them is the same as showing contempt for God's kindness, forbearance, and patience. That's because, instead of allowing God's mercy to compel us to fall before him and admit our own bankruptcy, we become prideful and try to judge ourselves by comparison to those we think are more sinful. I have a news flash for you: you are not superior to other sinners in any way. If anything separates us from them, it is only that God has mercifully allowed us into his kingdom because of our repentance and his mercy. That's it! That's all I or anyone else has going for them. How can I be morally superior when the only reason I'm okay with God is because he's already paid my tab? I strive to be moral, but I only do so because of what he's done for me, not because I think I can earn a spot in heaven by being good enough from now until the moment I die. But I can't ever be good enough, and if I ever thought I could get right with God by perfectly obeying his law, it only gets worse when I try to obey the secular laws that are in a constant state of flux.

When I'm banking on worldly codes of morality, I'm banking on something that is continually changing. I can't count on this code because fickle people dreamed it up. It's dangerous business, and this is at the heart of cancel culture. And it always has been.

If you are wondering what a shifting worldly moral code looks like in the twenty-first century, take a look at what happened to Seth Jahn in early 2021. He's a member of the US Soccer Federation's Athlete Council and a twice-wounded special forces veteran. Well, Seth was booted out of the group because while he was speaking in favor of keeping the US Soccer Federation's ban on kneeling during the playing of the national anthem, he said that anyone who disrespected the flag or the anthem was also disrespecting the sacrifice that soldiers have made in the wars and conflicts in which they fought to preserve our freedom. Then Jahn added that African Americans were not the only ethnic group to have a history of enslavement, but virtually every ethnicity throughout history had been victimized by some form of forced labor and chattel slavery. He then made a point that only one country in world history had ever fought a civil war to abolish the barbaric practice of human beings owning other human beings, and that refusing to stand for the national anthem was disrespectful to the hundreds of thousands of American soldiers who had shed their blood in that war for the freedom of enslaved Americans.[4]

I'm not going to argue for or against Jahn's point of view, but rather I want to concentrate on the rationale the US Soccer Federation used for expelling him from the council. Did they argue that his argument was invalid? Did they propose to have a discussion within their organization about the validity of his point of view. Nope. The only reason they offered for removing him from the council was that Jahn had "violated the Prohibited Conduct's Policy section on harassment, which prohibits racial and other harassment based upon a person's protected status (race), including any verbal act in which race is used or implied in a manner *which would make a reasonable person uncomfortable"* (emphasis added).[5]

Uncomfortable? Is that the new standard of morality? What does comfort have to do with anything, for crying out loud? This is like nailing Jell-O to the wall. Of course language can make us uncomfortable, especially when it challenges preconceived ideas about what is right or wrong. Can people grow and mature without feeling uncomfortable? Hardly, because it's human nature to fall back on our biases and prejudices. Letting go of long-held ideas and behaviors, no matter how wrong or pigheaded, can be extremely uncomfortable. For example, if someone drinks too much, would it be uncomfortable for her if her family staged an intervention to convince her to seek help? When my boys were in school and their grades were slipping, do you think they were comfortable with my scolding? I think you know the answer to that.

I argue that canceling a fellow member of the human race for the simple fact they brought discomfort to someone else is a dangerous game. If that is the standard for deciding who is in and who is out, then everyone is in peril. Who can grow in their thinking? Who can progress? Who can ever overcome their past mistakes? Sometimes we have to say things out loud to discover how stupid our ideas are. Even worse, who can avoid the wrath of cancel culture if that's the yardstick we use? The answer is that no one can stand. It's an unkeepable law. It's the twenty-first-century equivalent of saying, "You hurt my feelings!"

Besides, isn't the US Soccer Federation guilty of the same crime? Didn't they violate their own law? Remember what Paul said in Romans: when you pass judgment, you are guilty too. Sometimes, you are guilty of the same thing you judged someone else for. Obviously, Jahn was uncomfortable with the language of those demanding the ban on kneeling be repealed. Do you think he was uncomfortable when they kicked him off the council? Did he get any consideration for his discomfort? Any bonus points because he felt uncomfortable? I don't think so. One could argue that Jahn's comments were tone deaf, that he failed to consider the emotionally charged social climate at the time. One might even argue his perspective was flawed with logical and factual errors. That would be fair. I have no issue with someone saying, "Hey, Seth, you're wrong and here's why."

But if language that causes others to feel uncomfortable is the standard we can use to cancel them, we are in serious trouble. This standard is too vague and relies too much on feelings and opinions to allow us to ever have a discussion that arrives at the truth. It's too fluid, too ambiguous. I need something more concrete, less open to interpretation if I am going to take the drastic step of calling someone out. In truth, anyone can fall into the trap of using language that makes others uncomfortable.

Unfortunately, this is the mud bog we dive into when we embrace the idea that we can guide our own steps. Without a moral standard rooted in eternity (which we get from God), we must make it up on the fly. Unfortunately, when we do that without God, common sense takes a hike. We become so muddle minded that we don't realize we just nailed a moral command to the wall that no one can keep. It leads to thinking so depraved that we don't realize that someone could turn the tables on us and use the same standard to cancel us. No one can live up to this because it is a double-edged sword that cuts us coming and going. That's what it's like when moral codes flow from depraved and wicked worldly minds. We just aren't qualified to do that.

This, America, is the main problem with cancel culture: it's based on a false morality. It's false because it relies on human constructs instead of the Word of an almighty, all-knowing, and all-powerful God. Do you think we might be better people if we understood what God meant when he said, "For I desire mercy, not sacrifice, and acknowledgment of God rather than burnt offerings" (Hos. 6:6)? Cancel culture condemns itself because it fails to consider God's desire that we admit we are all moral failures. It misses the point that we can only receive much-needed mercy by dispensing mercy ourselves.

Jesus addressed this issue in Matthew 18:21–22 (NLT). Peter was always trying to one-up the rest of the ragtag band of disciples. Here he came to Jesus with a question I suspect was crafted to make himself seem grandly benevolent: "Lord, how often should I forgive someone who sins against me? Seven times?" (v. 21). I'm sure Peter was thinking that Jesus would pat him on his self-righteous noggin and say, "You're amazing, Peter!" But far from congratulating Peter on his generosity, Jesus upped the ante by responding, "No, not seven times, but seventy times seven!" (v. 22). I don't know for sure, but I'm thinking Peter was shocked once he did the math. "Let's see, seven times zero is zero. Seven times seven is forty-nine. Four hundred ninety times! You've got to be kidding me, Jesus. Four hundred ninety times! That's a lot of forgiving!"

The Lord wanted Peter to understand mercy, so he concluded his mini sermon by telling a parable about a man who owed his king roughly two hundred years' worth of wages. When the king threatened to cast him into debtors' prison, the man begged for the king's mercy. The king took pity on him and forgave the entire debt. But later the king found out that this servant accosted a fellow servant and demanded payment for a very small debt. When that man begged for mercy, the unmerciful servant had the man thrown into debtors' prison until the bill was paid. When the king discovered his servant's failure to dispense the same mercy that had been granted to him, he called the servant wicked and unmerciful and had him imprisoned *and* tortured until he paid back all that he owed.

When people demand more from their neighbors than they themselves are able to deliver, the outcome before God is not good. God delights in pouring his grace and mercy on undeserving sinners such as you and me. We don't deserve it, but he gives it to us freely and joyfully. Hopefully, you see the application to cancel culture. Perhaps more than anything else demanded of us, God requires that we reflect his nature and character by being merciful and forgiving ourselves. And I know one thing: I don't want to be the wicked and unmerciful servant. That's why I avoid the temptation to engage in anything that smacks of unforgiveness. Another way of saying this is to treat others the way you'd want God to treat you (Matt. 6:12; Matt. 7:12). If you desire judgment and justice before God, then all I can say is, have at it. But before you go that route, I'd suggest you take inventory of your failures to keep the law of God perfectly. I'm much more into God's mercy because I'm completely aware of my many moral failures. That's why I try to forgive others before they even ask, since I want God to forgive me in the same way.

Just so you don't misunderstand and think I'm saying we should just ignore sinful behavior, let me be very clear: I condemn sinful behavior. I have no problem with doing that, but I don't operate in a vacuum. I don't just make stuff up as I go along. I don't know what moral code the world appeals to, but I know what my source of authority is. I rely on what God has revealed to me through his Word. I've already pointed out that the alternative to an all-powerful, all-knowing God who reveals morality to us is that we are on our own. If God's not there, and if he's not telling us how to live, then we have to put our hope and confidence in the goodness of other people. I don't know about you, but I've never yet met a human being I thought I could trust with that responsibility, including myself.

However, when I condemn sin, there is one glaring difference between what I do and what cancel culture does. My goal is not to condemn the sinner. I'm not out to destroy anyone. For one thing, I don't have the authority to do that. As I said, I'm too flawed and sinful myself. Instead, my goal is to do whatever I can to convince others that they are on the brink of destruction. Sin is an indicator that we've wandered away from God, who is the only one who can give us real life. If I want to be a part of canceling anything, I want to introduce sinners to the only one who can cancel their debt of sin and put them on the right path.

There are any number of behaviors I condemn, past and present (including my own). But the rationale for my condemnation isn't rooted in popular culture. It surely isn't rooted in the fear that what I say might make someone uncomfortable. Instead of pulling morality out of thin air, I look to the ultimate lawgiver when I'm searching for right and wrong. I want to know what he says because he does not change with the fickle winds of culture. People, on the other hand, can't make up their collective mind about good and evil. For them, today's virtue is tomorrow's sin.

But God is not like that. His morality is reliable because it flows from his mind. When I cast my eyes and thoughts on the enormity and complexity of creation, I'm aware of the fact that the God who did all of this is too great for me to ever understand. Then, when I read his Word and realize I am the object of his affection, I know I can trust what he tells me about morality. I have no doubts. None!

But when I think of the thousands of people I've ever known, I can't think of a single one of them I would trust to impart that kind of wisdom to me. My mother and father tried to teach me morality, but they did so by pointing to the Creator. Even then, I didn't take their word for it; I had to check it out for myself. I want to be sure that I open-mindedly read his message to humanity because he is the only one I have confidence in.

It might make you uncomfortable when I tell you that I don't trust you. Don't feel bad; I don't trust myself either. Not when it comes to God's law. If you're wondering why I'm always skeptical of human reasoning, it is because "there is a way that appears to be right, but in the end it leads to death" (Prov. 16:25). None of us is qualified to determine right from wrong because we have both a predisposition to take the wrong turn and to believe the wrong thing. I know that evil thoughts lurk in my heart. And from what I read in the Bible and from what I know about the people I've met, we are all just alike. We can't trust one another. Not with something as important as this, we can't.

But I can trust God because "the law of the LORD is perfect, refreshing the soul. The statutes of the LORD are trustworthy, making wise the simple" (Ps. 19:7). King David said the law of the Lord has the capacity to make "wise the simple." Another translation says the law of the Lord is "dependable. It makes gullible people wise" (GW).

Someone told me I should get in touch with my inner self. And I'm in touch with my inner self, all right. And what I see when I look at my own heart scares the fire out of me! I see a gullible man who believes all too easily Satan's lies about morality. I am a sinful man, for sure. But when God's law was revealed to me to be perfect and trustworthy, it refreshed my soul. I saw a path forward to a place of purpose and healing. I saw a way out of the miry pit that had become my life. A once gullible man became wise, not by his own power or strength but by the power of his association with the law of the Lord.

My problem in my younger days was that I thought God was holding out on me. I assumed his commandments were designed to test my will and make life difficult for me. I imagined he was sitting on his throne with a holy flyswatter, ready to splatter my worthless hide as soon as I sinned. When people misunderstand God's nature and his purpose for them, this is the kind of junk they come up with.

Thankfully, God restored my failed vision and allowed me to catch frequent glimpses of who he really is. I finally saw that, instead of a flyswatter, God was working hard and sacrificially to restore my soul. He labored to make a fool wise. I finally understood why the apostle John said that God's commands shouldn't be a burden to me (1 John 5:3). I finally realized his commands are intended to relieve my burdens by providing a clear, lighted path for me to walk. God seemed to be saying, "Just trust me. Obey me. I promise you, everything I tell you to do is for your own benefit and for my glory. You can trust what I tell you."

On the other hand, the world loves to use the power of shame and guilt as a weapon to cancel people. When they do this, they certainly don't have anyone else's welfare at heart, because they don't have a reliable moral compass. Their morality is whatever they determine it should be, whatever gives them more power.

I'm not on social media for a very good reason, but from what I hear, one thought comes to mind: some folks like to present themselves as authorities on a wide range of topics. People who never attended medical school suddenly come across as experts on vaccines, viruses, and cancer treatments. Over the years, any number of rednecks and river rats have entered my home. Most of them are opinionated on a variety of topics, including medicine. If I had to guess, I suspect most of them never took biology in high school, much less passed it. Yet they are ever ready to share their medical knowledge with me.

Let me let you in on a little secret: when I have a medical issue, I don't scan Facebook for advice on how to treat my ailment. I don't consult my river-rat friends. Jimmy Red, my handyman, is an expert at repairing my equipment by using redneck technology, but I wouldn't trust him as far as I could throw him with a problem with my health. No, when I have a medical issue, I load up my rig and head to the office of a highly trained physician.

When it comes to my relationship with God and living the moral life he wants me to live, I'm not entrusting anyone with that responsibility. I want to hear it from the expert of all experts, from the one who created me. I want to read it in the owner's manual, the Word of God:

> For the Word of God is alive and active. Sharper than any double-edged sword, it penetrates even to dividing soul and spirit, joints and marrow; it judges the thoughts and attitudes of the heart. (Heb. 4:12)

You'll have to decide for yourself who you are going to go with when it comes to figuring out what is right or wrong. Either you'll go with God or you'll follow the world's false and fickle moral codes. As for me, I'm going with the only one I trust. I'm going with God. If you want my advice, I suggest you listen to what Joshua told the Hebrews some three thousand years ago. I suggest you decide how you are going to live. Make a decision. When you choose God, you've chosen clarity over confusion, because you've chosen the God who has no beginning and no end. He is the Alpha and the Omega, the beginning and the end. You've chosen the reliable over the unreliable. Trust me when I tell you, you won't regret it:

> Choose for yourselves this day whom you will serve, whether the gods your ancestors served beyond the Euphrates, or the gods of the Amorites, in whose land you are living. But as for me and my household, we will serve the LORD. (Josh. 24:15)

So far the Almighty has led me in the right direction. He has never once let me down. I think I'll stick with him the rest of the way.

THE GOSPEL: WE ARE UNASHAMED

When I am afraid, I put my trust in you.
In God, whose word I praise—
in God I trust and am not afraid.
What can mere mortals do to me?
Psalm 56:3–4

No doubt about it, the world is a whacked-up place. Still, as I've said several times, I am a man of hope, so you won't find me squandering what precious few years I have left on this planet wringing my hands and wishing I was living in a perfect world. In fact, I accept the fact that I live on a sin-cursed planet and that it will be cursed until the day the Lord Jesus Christ returns in his resurrected glory to heal all brokenness. I'll work hard to improve conditions here on earth, but at the end of the day, that's not my ultimate goal. What I'm really after is to snatch as many people as I can from the fires of destruction that cause them to be filled with fear and confusion. I'm trying to pull as many as I can into the kingdom of God. I do this because I know that only in Christ can mankind find true clarity.

> Be merciful to those who doubt; save others by snatching them from the fire; to others show mercy, mixed with fear. (Jude vv. 22–23)

You might ask, "With all the evil in the world, how can you be so joyful? Aren't you afraid?" I mentioned this earlier, but you wouldn't believe the battle gear I'm wearing. I'm not talking about Kevlar or semiautomatic weapons or anything like that. Oh, trust me, I have plenty of such weapons and know how to use them. A reporter once asked me how long it would take the Ouachita Parish sheriff's office to get a deputy to my house after

I dialed 911. My reply was, "Out here in this neck of the woods, *I am* 911." But while those arms may protect me from a crazed intruder, they won't arm me for the real battle, that is, the spiritual battle for the souls of humanity. For that battle, I have the full armor of God (Eph. 6:10–20).

Were it not for the Almighty outfitting me for battle, I'd go down in flames on Satan's first wave of attack. Think about it. My bulletproof armor is a belt of truth and a breastplate of righteousness. When a person like me turns away from wickedness and turns to the giver of life, God makes him invincible, gives him immortality. His life becomes dedicated to truth seeking and righteousness, the kind of righteousness that doesn't begin with himself (Phil. 3:9) but is a gift from God. Once I turned away from myself and began to pursue my heavenly Father, my feet were shod with the latest in spiritual footwear that enabled me to respond at a moment's notice to anything that sets itself up against the knowledge of God. I am permanently in DEFCON 1, ready to spread the news that God has made peace with mankind through the sacrifice of Christ on the cross.

Yes, since the day I put on Christ's armor, I've been steadily proclaiming his name. Fortunately for me, I've also been surrounded by spiritual brothers and sisters to help me accomplish the task God has given me. When I first became one with Christ, I desperately sought out the wisdom of older believers to serve as mentors. Our pastor, Bill Smith, poured the Word of God into me and prepared me to preach the name of Jesus unapologetically and unashamedly. I also partnered with other new Christians, like Mac Owen, who had just been redeemed from a years-long addiction to crystal meth. We spurred one another on to take Jesus to the broken people in our community who were living as we had been living, begging them to give it all up for the sake of Christ.

Before too long we had a ragtag band of like-minded folks who wanted to take the message of the gospel to our little part of the world. We ate together, played together, studied the Scriptures together, and worshipped together. It was not uncommon to find our house packed with river rats, drunks, addicts, prostitutes, and other misfits every night of the week. When one of us suffered a loss, we all mourned. When one of us was ill, the rest of the group fed their family. When one of us faced opposition for preaching the name of Jesus, we all gathered and reminded that person that he not only had a family to support him but he also had the armor of God that would enable him to fight the battle successfully.

Perhaps most important of all, when one of our band was being tormented by Satan with the lie that they had exhausted God's love, we reminded them that God's promise was real, God's love was so steadfast it never ceases, it never comes to an end. Regardless of what went on today, he will renew us in the morning.

> The steadfast love of the LORD never ceases;
>> his mercies never come to an end;
> they are new every morning;
>> great is your faithfulness. (Lam. 3:22–23 ESV)

What's amazing is that nearly fifty years later, most of us who are still alive are still at it, still telling people about Jesus and his grace, still practicing hospitality, still laying it all down for the sake of the kingdom, still doing it together, even if we are doing it in different parts of the world. We are still a team to this day.

And let us consider how we may spur one another on toward love and good deeds, not giving up meeting together, as some are in the habit of doing, but encouraging one another—and all the more as you see the Day approaching. (Heb. 10:24–25)

I'd never heard the following phrase until the pandemic of 2020, but it's a good one to give you an idea of what our lives have been like since we joined forces all those years ago to bring God's kingdom to our community: we developed a *herd immunity.* And a herd we were, like a bunch of wild animals who had just escaped Satan's grasp by the skin of our teeth. If you'd seen us gathered as a group, your first response would have been to assume a wild drinking, dope-smoking, sexually immoral party was about to break out. But even though we didn't look much like church folk, we did our best to live out the scripture I quoted above: to encourage one another, to spur one another on to love and good deeds, to keep our focus on our Lord who has promised to return for us.

A herd? Oh, it was a herd all right. A mighty herd of God-worshiping, gospel-preaching, unashamed disciples of Jesus. And because of Jesus, we were immune to the virus that had once ravaged our bodies and souls. We were free from both the penalty and control of sin. A herd. All of us going in the same direction.

You may be thinking, "Yeah, that was all fine and good back in the hippie days, before everyone was on social media and trying to cancel everyone else out. I can't see that happening today."

I hate to burst your bubble, but it's still going on today. Besides, do you think people weren't resisting the gospel in the late 1970s and early 1980s? Trust me when I tell you they were. Resistance to the gospel is as old as the gospel itself. This cancel culture business is nothing new; it's just a little more potent because of social media and the internet today. But it's always been there. Long before the internet became a thing, I was threatened with violence when Miss Kay and I rescued a woman who had been abused by her partner. An angry brother unloaded a boxload of roofing tacks on our road, ruining every tire on every one of our vehicles. I've been vilified in the press and accused of all kinds of evil. Mercifully, God has so far allowed us to remain faithful because we have that band of disciples that encourages us to stay focused on Jesus.

I guess we could have done it by ourselves, but I don't see how. Having a community of like-minded folks all these years has empowered us in two ways. One, when we were guilty of what we were accused of, we weren't allowed to wallow in self-pity and shame. Our family, our brothers and sisters, have always been faithful in pointing out to us that *the steadfast love of the Lord never ceases, that his mercies are new every morning.* Guilt and shame never had an opportunity to take root in my heart because my family of believers was always there to snatch it out like a weed before it could grow. Second, whenever we were falsely accused, we were there to remind one another that opposition goes with the territory. We reminded one another of scriptures such as:

Blessed are those who are persecuted because of righteousness, for theirs is the kingdom of heaven. Blessed are you when people insult you, persecute you and falsely say all kinds of evil against you because of me. Rejoice and be glad, because great is your reward in heaven, for in the same way they persecuted the prophets who were before you. (Matt. 5:10–12)

If the world hates you, keep in mind that it hated me first. If you belonged to the world, it would love you as its own. As it is, you do not belong to the world, but I have chosen you out of the world. That is why the world hates you. Remember what I told you: "A servant is not greater than his master." If they persecuted me, they will persecute you also. If they obeyed my teaching, they will obey yours also. They will treat you this way because of my name, for they do not know the one who sent me. (John 15:18–21)

Do we think we can escape the world's anger if we are proposing a different worldview that challenges what they believe, which is the idea that we can be good on our own? Can we escape judgment if we proclaim from the mountaintops that we are in desperate need of a savior? Think about it. When you first heard the gospel, did you drop what you were doing and run after Jesus with reckless abandon? Perhaps some of you did, and I envy you. If I had done that, I would have saved myself a lot of trouble. But most of us found the gospel grated on our nerves because the gospel assumes our guilt, and who wants to find out that our guilt is the reason the Son of God had to die?

Yes, persecution and opposition go hand in hand with walking with Jesus. When we follow him, there's always the threat of it. I'm not saying we should seek it out or even that we should enjoy it. It always carries a certain amount of pain when someone tries to cancel us, I don't care who you are. But we should not be surprised when it happens. How do I know that? God said so:

Dear friends, do not be surprised at the fiery ordeal that has come on you to test you, as though something strange were happening to you. But rejoice inasmuch as you participate in the sufferings of Christ, so that you may be overjoyed when his glory is revealed. If you are insulted because of the name of

Christ, you are blessed, for the Spirit of glory and of God rests on you. If you suffer, it should not be as a murderer or thief or any other kind of criminal, or even as a meddler. However, if you suffer as a Christian, do not be ashamed, but praise God that you bear that name. (1 Peter 4:12–16)

Did you get that? This is what I'm talking about. Don't be shocked. If you are speaking the truth of the gospel and you are speaking it in love, what do you have to be ashamed of? The answer is *nothing*! Do you see anything in this passage that suggests you have a right to preach without ridicule or opposition? Without threats of violence or confiscation of your property? I'm afraid not! Instead, Peter encouraged us to *rejoice* when we are persecuted because it connects us with Christ. If you are insulted for Christ's sake, count your blessings. It means that God's Spirit rests on you. Overall, do not be ashamed, but clap your hands and jump for joy that you wear the name of God.

The cultural Christian—the one who just punches his church attendance clock—is not going to want to hear this. But if you're serious about the kingdom of God and if you're serious about following Jesus, this should fire you up. That's because seeing cancel culture for what it is should be liberating. It should remove all fear and shame and embolden you to preach the gospel in love to a lost world that desperately needs to hear it. After all, someone's life depends on it.

Yes, we are a mighty herd that is immune to whatever those in opposition to us are trying to dish out. We are immune because we follow the one who paid for our immunity with his blood. It's easy to feel as if you're fighting alone, but you should know there are millions of us out there preaching in the name of Christ and trying to persuade people to turn away from their sins and give control of their lives over to Jesus. You are not alone. Besides that, when you have the cure for what really ails people, you should never be ashamed of that. You have been given the words of life. Now go and share them with the people who need it most.

> I am obligated both to Greeks and non-Greeks, both to the wise and the foolish. That is why I am so eager to preach the gospel also to you who are in Rome. For I am not ashamed of the gospel, because it is the power of God that brings salvation to everyone who believes. (Rom. 1:14–16)

Our broken culture presents me with a choice: either I can obsess about the cruelty and heartlessness of the culture that seeks to devour and destroy or I can put my hope in Jesus. He is the ultimate canceler, but he alone cancels those things that would destroy me:

- He cancels my cancellation
- He cancels my guilt and shame
- He cancels my addiction to worldly systems
- He cancels my fear of the unknown
- He cancels my confusion
- He cancels false morality

On top of all of that, when we put our trust in him, he gives all of us who trust him herd immunity from the disease of hopelessness. This is as good as it gets. God dropped a nuclear bomb on Satan when he raised Jesus from the hole in the ground. So now, no matter how bleak the future may seem to be in America today, God is in charge of everything that is really important. Because of what Jesus did, I am now free from sin, free from the grave, and free from condemnation. If God approves of me based on my belief that Jesus is risen from the dead, what can another person do to me? The answer is clear. Nobody can lay a glove on me. I'm immune to all of that junk now. All of it! For that reason, I don't spend a lot of time worrying about culture. I'm too busy telling folks about Jesus.

You can be free of it too. Wherever I go, I encourage folks to lay down their toys and trinkets and follow Jesus. I plead with them to follow the one who has put the Evil One on notice that his days are numbered. He will come after you and me, but I'm walking with Jesus, and I'm walking with you, so we are good to go. We are immune because of the blood of Christ. It's a pretty good deal, if you ask me. If you have a better one, I'd like to know about it.

NOTES

Preface

1. Samantha Kubota, "James Cordon Responds to Petition Calling for End to Segment Mocking Asian Foods," *TODAY*, June 10, 2021, https://www.today.com/food/petition-calls-james-corden-end-spill-your-guts-segment-t221575.
2. Neil MacFarquhar, "With Homicides Rising, Cities Brace for a Violent Summer," *New York Times*, June 1, 2021, https://www.nytimes.com/2021/06/01/us/shootings-in-us.html.
3. https://www.businessinsider.com/burger-king-chicken-sandwich-shooting-spicy-sauce-restaurant-memphis-tennessee-2021-6.

Chapter 1: What Is Cancel Culture?

1. Jeremy Krail, "Drew Brees Apologizes for 'Insensitive' Comments on National Anthem Protests," WBRZ, June 4, 2020, https://www.wbrz.com/news/drew-brees-i-will-never-agree-with-anyone-disrespecting-the-flag-/.
2. J. K. Rowling (@jk_rowling), Twitter, June 6, 2020, 5:35 p.m., https://twitter.com/jk_rowling/status/1269382518362509313?lang=en.
3. Eliza Skinner (@elizaskinner), June 6, 2020, 5:56 p.m., reply to Rowling, https://twitter.com/elizaskinner/status/1269387766506254336?lang=en.
4. Pixelatedboat aka "Mr. Tweets" (@pixelatedboat), June 6, 2020, 6:20 p.m., reply to Rowling, https://twitter.com/pixelatedboat/status/1269393764788789248?lang=en.
5. Emma Nolan, "What Happened with Chris Pratt? Twitter Poll Launches a Week of Backlash," *Newsweek*, October 21, 2020, https://www.newsweek.com/chris-pratt-backlash-twitter-poll-politics-religion-animals-1540991.

6. Nico Lang, "Masterpiece Cakeshop Owner in Court Again for Denying LGBTQ Customer," NBC News, April 15, 2020, https://www.nbcnews.com/feature/nbc-out/masterpiece-cakeshop-owner-court-again-denying-lgbtq-customer-n1184656.

7. Sarah Pulliam Bailey, "Secret Recordings, Leaked Letters: Explosive Secrets Rocking the Southern Baptist Convention," *Washington Post*, June 12, 2021, https://www.washingtonpost.com/religion/2021/06/12/southern-baptist-convention-secret-infighting-meeting/.

8. Michael Costello (@MichaelCostello), Instagram, June 14, 2021, in Lindsay Weinberg, "Fashion Designer Michael Costello Says He Had Suicidal Thoughts After Alleged Chrissy Teigen Bullying," Yahoo!, June 14, 2021, https://www.yahoo.com/now/fashion-designer-michael-costello-says-001700509.html.

9. Scott Stump, "Designer Says He Has Ongoing Suicidal Thoughts Years After Exchanges with Chrissy Teigen," *TODAY*, June 15, 2021, https://www.today.com/popculture/designer-michael-costello-has-suicidal-thoughts-years-after-exchanges-chrissy-t222122.

Chapter 2: Where Did Cancel Culture Come From?

1. Chris Green, "Dennis the Menace Is Now Just Plain Dennis as Part of Rebrand," *i* (news), December 27, 2017, https://inews.co.uk/news/uk/dennis-menace-now-just-plain-dennis-part-rebrand-113278.

2. "Advert for 'Reliable' Worker 'Rejected' by Jobcentre," BBC News, January 27, 2010, http://news.bbc.co.uk/2/hi/uk_news/england/norfolk/8483171.stm.

3. Gouverneur Morris, "Preamble," Interactive Constitution, September 17, 1787, https://constitutioncenter.org/interactive-constitution/preamble.

4. Perry Chiaramonte, "Michigan Dubs Birthplace of 1960's Radical Movement Official Historical Site," FOX News, January 11, 2015, last updated June 22, 2017, https://www.foxnews.com/us/michigan-dubs-birthplace-of-1960s-radical-movement-official-historical-site.

5. Tom Hayden, *The Port Huron Statement* (New York: Students for

a Democratic Society, 1962), 4, https://images2.americanprogress
.org/campus/email/PortHuronStatement.pdf.

6. Dinitia Smith, "No Regrets for a Love of Explosives; in a Memoir
of Sorts, a War Protester Talks of Life with the Weathermen,"
New York Times, September 11, 2001, https://www.nytimes
.com/2001/09/11/books/no-regrets-for-love-explosives-memoir
-sorts-war-protester-talks-life-with.html.

7. Hayden, *The Port Huron Statement*, 4.

8. Alexander A. Plateris, *Divorces and Divorce Rates*, National
Vital Statistics System 21, no. 29 (1978; repr., Hayattsville, MD:
U.S. Department of Health, Education, and Welfare, 1980), 5,
https://www.cdc.gov/nchs/data/series/sr_21/sr21_029.pdf.

9. CDC/NCHS National Vital Statistics System, *Provisional
Number of Marriages and Marriage Rate: United States,
2000–16*, https://www.cdc.gov/nchs/data/dvs/national_marriage
_divorce_rates_00-16.pdf.

10. Theodore Caplow, Louis Hicks, and Ben J. Wattenberg, "Family:
Nonmarital Births," chap. 4 in *The First Measured Century*
(Washington, DC: AEI Press, 2000), https://www.pbs.org/fmc
/book/4family10.htm.

11. Frederic Michas, "Percentage of Births to Unmarried Women in
the U.S.: 1980–2019," Statistica, May 28, 2021, https://www
.statista.com/statistics/276025/us-percentage-of-births-to
-unmarried-women/.

12. John Winthrop, "A Modell of Christian Charity (1630),"
Collections of the Massachusetts Historical Society, 3rd series
(Boston: Massachusetts Historical Society, 1838), 47, in the
Hanover Historical Texts Collection, https://history.hanover.edu
/texts/winthmod.html.

13. "Declaration of Independence: A Transcription," National
Archives, July 4,, 1776, https://www.archives.gov/founding-docs
/declaration-transcript.

14. John Adams to Massachusetts Militia, October 11, 1798, in
Founders Online, National Archives, https://founders.archives
.gov/documents/Adams/99-02-02-3102.

Chapter 3: Who Participates in Cancel Culture?

1. Louis L'Amour, *Mojave Crossing* (1964; repr., New York: Bantam Books, 2015), 51.
2. Joe Hagan, "'So Many Great, Educated, Functional People Were Brainwashed': Can Trump's Cult of Followers Be Deprogrammed?", *Vanity Fair*, January 21, 2021, https://www.vanityfair.com /news/2021/01/can-trumps-cult-of-followers-be-deprogrammed.
3. Elizabeth Elizalde, "White Teen Pushed Out of College After Video of Her Saying N-Word at 15 Resurfaces," *New York Post*, December 29, 2020, https://nypost.com/2020/12/29/white-teen -kicked-out-of-college-after-n-word-video-resurfaces/.
4. Justin Curto, "Teen Vogue Editor-in-Chief Backs Out Over Anti-Asian Tweets," Vulture, March 18, 2021, https://www.vulture .com/2021/03/teen-vogue-new-editor-alexi-mccammond-racist -tweets.html.

Chapter 4: Why Is Cancel Culture Happening?

1. Oprah Winfrey, "Oprah Winfrey's Cecil B. DeMille Award Acceptance Speech" (76th Golden Globe Awards, The Beverly Hilton, Beverly Hills, California, January 6, 2019), video shared by NBC, December 30, 2019, on YouTube, https://www.youtube .com/watch?v=TTyiq-JpM-0&ab_channel=NBC.
2. *American Dictionary of the English Language*, s.v. "truth," http://webstersdictionary1828.com/Dictionary/truth.
3. *Cambridge Dictionary*, s.v. "truth," https://dictionary.cambridge .org/us/dictionary/english/truth.
4. Jeff Selle and Maureen Dolan, "Black Like Me?" *Coeur d'Alene Press*, June 11, 2015, https://cdapress.com/news/2015/jun/11 /black-like-me-5/.
5. Sam Dorman, "An Estimated 62 Million Abortions Have Occurred Since Roe v. Wade Decision in 1973," Fox News, January 22, 2021, https://www.foxnews.com/politics/abortions -since-roe-v-wade.

Chapter 5: Who's the Boss?

1. GracePointe Church, "As Progressive Christians, we're open to the tensions and inconsistencies of the Bible," Facebook Photo,

February 7, 2021, https://m.facebook.com/gracepointetn/photos
/a.394837242014/10157495440607015/?type=3.

Chapter 6: There's a Vaccine for That!

1. Constance Grady, "Ellen DeGeneres, George W. Bush, and the
Death of Uncritical Niceness," Vox, October 9, 2019, https://
www.vox.com/culture/2019/10/9/20906371/ellen-degeneres
-george-w-bush-controversy.
2. Naomi LaChance, "Ellen Staunchly Defends Her Nauseating
Friendship with George W. Bush," Splinter, October 8, 2019,
https://splinternews.com/ellen-staunchly-defends-her-nauseating
-friendship-with-1838864797.

Chapter 8: Check Your Passport

1. Maria Sacchetti, "U.S.-Mexico Border Apprehensions for the
Fiscal Year Surpassed 1 Million in June," The Texas Tribune,
July 16, 2021, https://www.texastribune.org/2021/07/16/us
-mexico-border-apprehensions-how-many/.

Chapter 9: I Ain't Afraid of No Ghosts!

1. C. S. Lewis, *The Weight of Glory* (New York: HarperOne, 2001),
26

Chapter 11: Who Are You to Tell Me What to Do?

1. Isla Grey, "Rock & Roll Scandal—Jerry Lee Lewis," BellaOnline,
accessed September 20, 2021, https://www.bellaonline.com
/articles/art4655.asp.
2. "Ingrid Bergman Gets Apology for Senate Attack," *New York
Times*, August 29, 1972, https://www.nytimes.com/1972/04/29
/archives/ingrid-bergman-gets-apology-for-senate-attack.html.
3. Deb Kiner, "'Duck Dynasty' Patriarch Phil Robertson Had an
Affair and Discovers He Has a Daughter: Report," Penn Live,
May 29, 2020, https://www.pennlive.com/entertainment/2020
/05/duck-dynasty-patriarch-phil-robertson-had-an-affair-and
-discovers-he-has-a-daughter-report.html.
4. Kenya Brown, "Seth Jahn Removed from U.S. Soccer Athlete's
Council After Racially-Charged Rant," SBI, March 1, 2021,

https://sbisoccer.com/2021/03/seth-jahn-removed-from-u-s
-soccer-athletes-council-after-racially-charged-rant.

5. Chris Ahrens (@chrisahrens), "Statement from the Athlete
   Council regarding Seth Jahn," Twitter, February 28, 2021,
   https://twitter.com/chrisahrens/status/1366219993940025345.

ABOUT THE AUTHOR

Phil Robertson is a professional hunter who invented his own duck call and founded the successful Duck Commander Company. He also starred in the popular television series on A&E, *Duck Dynasty*, and is now the cohost of the hugely popular podcast, *Unashamed with Phil & Jase Robertson*. He is a *New York Times* bestselling author of *Jesus Politics*; *The Theft of America's Soul*; *Happy, Happy, Happy*; and *UnPHILtered*. He and his wife, Kay, live in West Monroe, Louisiana. He has five children, nineteen grandchildren, and thirteen great-grandchildren.